T0329009

Cambridge Elements ≡

Elements in Religion and Violence
edited by
James R. Lewis
University of Tromsø
and
Margo Kitts
Hawai'i Pacific University

BEYOND BRAINWASHING

Perspectives on Cult Violence

Rebecca Moore

CAMBRIDGE
UNIVERSITY PRESS

CAMBRIDGE
UNIVERSITY PRESS

University Printing House, Cambridge CB2 8BS, United Kingdom

One Liberty Plaza, 20th Floor, New York, NY 10006, USA

477 Williamstown Road, Port Melbourne, VIC 3207, Australia

314–321, 3rd Floor, Plot 3, Splendor Forum, Jasola District Centre,
New Delhi – 110025, India

79 Anson Road, #06–04/06, Singapore 079906

Cambridge University Press is part of the University of Cambridge.

It furthers the University's mission by disseminating knowledge in the pursuit of
education, learning, and research at the highest international levels of excellence.

www.cambridge.org
Information on this title: www.cambridge.org/9781108448314
DOI: 10.1017/9781108646598

First published 2018

A catalogue record for this publication is available from the British Library.

ISBN 978-1-108-44831-4 Paperback
ISSN 2397-9496 (online)
ISSN 2514-3786 (print)

Cambridge Elements

Beyond Brainwashing
Perspectives on Cult Violence

Rebecca Moore

ABSTRACT: This analysis reviews the state of the question regarding theories of cult violence. It introduces definitions and vocabulary and presents relevant historical examples of religious violence. It then discusses the 1960s and 1970s, the period immediately before the Jonestown tragedy. Considerations of events after Jonestown (1978) and Waco (1993) follow. Subsequent to 9/11 (2001), some of the themes identified in previous decades reappear. The book concludes by examining the current problem of repression and harassment directed at religious believers. Legal discrimination by governments, as well as persecution of religious minorities by non-state actors, has challenged earlier fears about cult violence.

KEYWORDS: cults, violence, New Religious Movements, brainwashing, Anticult Movement

ISBNs: 9781108448314 PB, 9781108646598 OC
ISSNs: 2397-9496 (online), 2514-3786 (print)

Contents

1 Introduction

At one point during the late twentieth century, the words "cult" and "violence" were practically interchangeable. New religions were seen as inherently dangerous and abusive, fraught with peril for the unwary college student or depressed housewife. Led by charlatans out to bilk gullible but well-meaning individuals, these religious groups succeeded only by brainwashing their victims through coercive practices. The violence inflicted on group members persuaded them to inflict violence upon outsiders as well as upon themselves. The mass murders and suicides in Jonestown, Guyana, in 1978 seemed only to confirm these apprehensions. The decade of the 1980s saw a spate of books and articles alerting the public to the perils of New Religious Movements, or NRMs.

But in 1993, a deadly clash between federal agents and members of the Branch Davidians, an offshoot of the Seventh-day Adventist denomination, prompted new considerations of the connection between cults and outbreaks of collective violence. In that case, it was clear that a contest between the group and outside forces hastened the tragic ending in which more than seventy Branch Davidians died in a blaze ignited in their communal quarters. As a result, a number of comparative studies from the 1990s emphasized the interaction between NRMs and their opponents. Additional disasters – such as the murders and suicides of the Solar Temple, the sarin gas attack in Tokyo by Aum Shinrikyō, and the suicides by members of Heaven's Gate – challenged both simplistic accounts and scholarly analyses by highlighting the manifold expressions of cult violence.

Then another disaster altered the course of scholarly appraisals of violence and new religions: the terror attacks of 11 September 2001 in the United States. Scholars had been discussing the rise of Islamism for decades (e.g., Esposito 1983; Arjomand 1984), but 9/11 shifted the attention from violence caused by members of NRMs to that practiced by adherents of radical Islam.

These three pivotal moments – Jonestown, Waco, and 9/11 – have driven research into the link between violence and New Religious Movements. The purpose of these investigations has always been in the cause of prediction and prevention: How can such explosive events be averted? What are the telltale signs and markers? What steps can be taken preemptively to avoid future tragedies? Despite countless studies written over the course of half a century, we always seem surprised when violence erupts.

Nevertheless, two very general conclusions have emerged from these examinations. The first is that violent behavior stems from several features internal to the group. These causes seem to include an apocalyptic or millennialist ideology that marks off strict boundaries between believers and nonbelievers, a charismatic leader who inspires followers, and a totalistic form of organization that isolates members within an encapsulated community. This configuration is not foolproof, for, as Barkun observed, "it is always possible to find non-violent groups that are, for example, led by charismatic leaders, physically isolated and doctrinally rigid" (Barkun 2004, 57).

The second, and related, conclusion is that those outside, rather than inside, the group may provoke violence. These "cultural opponents" usually comprise relatives and former group members, the news media, and government agencies (Hall 1987). In other words, violence does not occur apart from a dynamic interaction between the group and hostile outsiders. What differentiates the assorted theories is the comparative weight academics give to the competing rationales: Is it the charismatic leader? Is it group isolation? Is it forceful adversaries? The answer to all of these questions is yes, depending on which group is being considered. Most recently, however, the role that state actors play in fomenting deadly outbursts has taken center stage and has aroused concern about the erosion of religious freedom around the world.

This historiographical analysis reviews the state of the question regarding theories of cult violence, going beyond the explanations visible in popular culture. It begins by introducing definitions and vocabulary to be used throughout and briefly reviews relevant historical examples of religious violence that predate the rise of concern about cults. It then discusses the 1960s and 1970s, the period immediately "Before Jonestown" in which a divide between scholarly and popular appraisals of new religions becomes apparent. Considerations of the post-Jonestown, and then post-Waco, literature follow. After 9/11, some of the themes identified in the 1960s and 1970s reappear – namely the contribution of apocalyptic expectations in justifying and contributing to the use of lethal force to achieve millennial goals. An appendix summarizes the major theories presented.

This book concludes by broaching the current apprehension regarding violence and religion – that is, the problem of repression and harassment directed at religious believers. Legal discrimination by governments, as well as persecution of religious minorities by non-state actors, has intensified dramatically. While safeguarding the religious rights of individuals has always been a concern, the defense of members of minority religions seems to have grown paramount.

2 Some Caveats and Definitions

We have only to look at daily news feeds to see the apparent bond between religion and violence. Moreover, this tie seems to be nothing new in religious history. Armstrong (2014) details many such instances in *Fields of Blood*. The scope of this book is more modest. First, it limits the consideration of violence to that perpetrated by New Religions Movements rather than by large, normative religious groups. Second, it excludes the 2,000-year-old history of apocalyptic violence, focusing instead on the late twentieth and early twenty-first centuries. Third, it does not encompass all forms of violence, but concentrates on just two: murder and suicide.

A few definitions and explanations are in order. Using the scholarly term New Religious Movement, or NRM, rather than the popular expression "cult," the book encompasses a variety of types of groups. (The word cult will be utilized as a convenience at times, though not in a pejorative sense, *pace* Rosedale, Langone, Bradshaw, and Eichel [2015].) They may be truly new – that is, appearing *de novo* in the past two centuries, such as the Church of Scientology or the Raelians. They may be new to a particular culture, planted by missionaries, gurus, or messiahs in foreign soil, such as Transcendental Meditation or Sōka Gakkai in Western cultures or Pentecostalism in Asian societies. They may be sectarian alternatives to mainstream religious forms, such as the Watchtower Society (Jehovah's Witnesses) or the Church of Jesus Christ of Latter-day Saints (Mormons). This book also includes under the NRM rubric emergent spiritualities claiming an ancient heritage, like the New Age and Paganism.

Another defining characteristic for an NRM is its departure from society's customs and traditions, which may create tension with the general cultural values of its environment. Writing from an explicitly Christian perspective, Martin saw cults as "a religion apart from the norm in our culture" (Martin 1965, 11). Even though the United States and Europe are religiously plural, Christianity is assumed to be normative; similarly, Islam has normative status in countries of the Middle East, while Hinduism dominates the Indian subcontinent. Therefore, NRM is a relative term: it might comprise any group that locates itself – or is placed by others – outside the religious mainstream of a particular society. Hostility to the movement's beliefs or practices may result from this outsider status.

In a global context, it is probably more precise to write of "minority religions" or "marginal religions" than of NRMs, since some groups may not be new to a society – e.g., Muslims in Burma or Christians in Saudi Arabia. But the different rituals and dogmas, frequently reflecting customs of ethnic sub-groups within the wider society, set them apart from the status quo and make them viable scapegoats on whom to blame social ills. The pressures created by ethnoreligious suspicion and quarrels very well resemble some clashes between NRMs and their host societies. In addition, groups traditionally classified as NRMs, such as the Church of Scientology or The Family International, have sustained the same kinds of restrictions and attacks as other minority religions. Consequently, I will be using these terms somewhat interchangeably.

Because injurious behavior can be physical, verbal, or written (Jackman 2002), it is necessary to clarify what is meant by violence in the context of this volume. A large body of literature details the psychological abuse and destructive behavior that cult leaders and members exhibit. For example, Moore (2011) details four types of violence that existed within Peoples Temple: discipline, behavior modification, behavior control, and terror. This book will not cover these areas and instead employs the word *violence* "to refer to intentional homicide or intentional suicide initiated within a religious group" (Levi 1982a, 6) or, put another way, "actions that are aimed at taking human life – that intend to, and do, kill" (Juergensmeyer 1988, 177). The violence under-taken is collective, rather than individualistic, and serves the ideology of the group, whether a religious organization or a control agency, such as the police or the military (Melton and Bromley 2009). Finally, and related to these definitions, is the theatrical aspect of the violence: its symbolic, rather than strategic, impact upon the hoped-for audience on the world stage. Juergensmeyer (1988) called this "performance violence," and though he was discussing acts of terror, the performative aspect of cult violence seems critical to its definition. Although other types of cult violence exist – such as intimidation of opponents outside the group or psychological, physical, and sexual coercion within the group – this book addresses only its perceptible manifestations. This is the kind of activity that affects public opinion and policy making.

This discussion, therefore, is interested in groups that use murder or suicide to obtain ideological ends. In this regard, Al-Rasheed and Shterin (2009) listed three primary and relevant actions: (1) sacrifice, that is, dying for a religious cause; (2) annihilating the self and the enemy, or many enemies, for the cause; and (3) annihilating others for the cause but not dying oneself. Instead of surveying the abuse that some groups practice to control their members, this book covers the violence that NRM members perpetrate against outsiders, along with self-directed violence, to achieve particular religious goals. (Self-immolation, such as that of Tibetan Buddhists today or Vietnamese Buddhists in the 1970s, might appear to warrant inclusion because it causes a sacrificial death pursued for political objectives. But since Buddhism is not an NRM in Tibet or Vietnam, this kind of violence will not be covered here.)

Because eschatological, apocalyptic, and millennial beliefs play a role in many instances of religious violence, an explanation of what is meant by those terms is needed. "Eschatology" simply means the study, or doctrine, of last things; this might refer to one's individual destiny after death or to the end of the world itself. Although an "apocalypse" is a genre of religious literature in which heavenly beings – angels, prophets, or human beings on cosmic journeys – reveal ultimate secrets, the term as understood today has a different meaning. It now generally refers to the cataclysmic end of the world in a final battle between good and evil. When we hear the word apocalyptic, we think of plagues, wars, pestilence, natural disasters, and other horrible trials that occur during this cosmic war.

"Millennialism," or "millenarianism," is "an academic term to refer to belief in an imminent transition to a collective salvation, in which the faithful will experience well-being and the unpleasant limitations of the human condition will be eliminated" (Wessinger 2011, 720). Based on the Christian belief in the return of Jesus Christ (Revelation 20), millennialism once referred strictly to the thousand-year reign of Christ on earth before the last battle between the righteous and the unrighteous. Today it encompasses almost any belief in shared deliverance, whether secular or religious, from the evils besetting the earth.

Emphasizing the differences between apocalypticism and millennialism may be drawing too fine a distinction between outlooks that have much in common. Apocalyptic believers hold that society is doomed, whereas millenarian believers postulate that the world will be transformed; but there are postapocalyptic groups that anticipate heaven on earth and other apocalyptic groups that expect a catastrophe to usher in a radical earthly change. Thus, some forms of apocalypticism unmistakably parallel millennial hopes for terrestrial salvation.

This terminology makes it difficult to identify acute differences between religious and political groups or to determine if violence stems from religious or political beliefs. According to Barkun (1974), distinctions between revolution/ politics and millenarianism/religion are mostly artificial. The slave revolt of 1831 inspired by Nat Turner (1800–1831), a religious visionary, nonetheless had enormous political repercussions, as did the prophetically driven, cattle-killing movement of 1856–1857 by the Xhosa tribe in South Africa. The very name "Christian Patriot" – those individuals in the United States arming themselves for an expected race war that will engage federal forces – combines the religious with the political. While millennial expectations frequently have political implications, this book emphasizes the NRMs that we consider as religious first and political second. This becomes rather complicated when we think about Islamist groups or Christian Reconstructionists who understand their respective religions to provide all-encompassing ways of life, without separating the sacred and secular.

3 Historical Cases

The tragedy in Jonestown of 1978 served as an important benchmark for scholarly assessments of violence and new religions (Melton and Bromley 2009). Attention shifted from historical apocalyptic movements and contemporary crises or protest cults to NRMs and their potential for slaughter. Because these precursors to the study of cult violence established a solid theoretical baseline for understanding the causes of extreme religious unrest, it is worth mentioning several key analysts and events.

The starting point for any consideration of religion and violence is René Girard, a French American historian and literary critic. Girard (1977) saw an intimate, and even causal, relationship between the two, with violence serving as the foundation of a religious order in which scapegoats simultaneously rid the community of its impurities and usher in its salvation. The surrogate victim required for collective cleansing need not be an individual, but may be a group, a nation, or even a race of people, such as "the Jews" or "the witches" who were blamed for the Black Death in medieval Europe (Girard 1986). Through the ritual of sacrificial purification, the community reestablished its boundaries and the threatened order was restored, for it was usually some sort of crisis that precipitated the violence. For example, Girard (2011) located the execution of Jesus within the context of the crisis of Roman-occupied Judea. We can see in our own day the relevance of Girard's scapegoat theories in the targeting of particular religious groups for exclusion or extermination.

Beyond Brainwashing

British historian Norman Cohn closely scrutinized occurrences of Christian millennial violence in Europe during the Middle Ages. His explanation of millenarian expectations – in which salvation is pictured as collective, terrestrial, imminent, total, and miraculous – continues to be utilized today (Cohn 1970, 15). Cohn identified a uniform historical context for the unbroken tradition of revolutionary millenarianism: epidemics of violence arose in "areas which were becoming seriously over-populated and were involved in a process of rapid economic and social change" (53). Many, if not most, of the participants in the popular crusades were poor and rootless, without land or employment, living on the margins, with leaders coming from the "lower strata of the intelligentsia" (85, 282). While some movements, like those of the Anabaptists, were egalitarian and relatively nonviolent, others, like those of Thomas Müntzer (d. 1525) who led the Peasant Revolt in Reformation-era Germany, justified violence on biblical grounds.

Michael Barkun updated and tested the theories put forward in *The Pursuit of the Millennium* in his own *Disaster and the Millennium* (1974), where he argued that social change by itself cannot account for explosions of millennial violence. Instead, he delineated four necessary conditions for the sudden appearance of beliefs in imminent terrestrial salvation, which may provoke lawlessness: multiple disasters (natural or human-caused), a body of ideas (that is, a coherent ideology), a charismatic leader, and a limited or concentrated disaster area (Barkun 1974, 6). Hunger, dispossession, war, and social upheaval may create the backdrop against which a sudden disaster – mild or dramatic – violently erupts. Barkun ended up where Cohn did, declaring that Stalinism and Nazism (he added Maoism) were contemporary forms of secular millennialism that could trace their lineages to earlier times.

Anthropologists extended the inquiry begun by historians and sociologists beyond the boundaries of Europe and the West by investigating the flare-ups of religious violence that occurred among tribal peoples and in non-

Western civilizations. Designated by many epithets – revitalization movements (Wallace 1956), messianic cults (Lanternari 1963), cargo cults (Worsley 1968), and crisis cults (La Barre 1971) – these movements shared a number of characteristics. Many arose in response to colonization or extreme oppression, or during times of intense social dislocation and transformation. Many had a charismatic leader who promised earthly salvation, either peacefully or by force. A number of movements sought a return to traditional ways of life, while others sought to overturn custom to enter an entirely new existence, either on earth or in a spiritual realm. Three historical cases exemplify the diversity that existed in the violence exhibited by these precursors to NRMs: the Taiping Rebellion in China (1850–1864), the Ghost Dance Movement in North America (1870–1890), and the twentieth-century cargo cults of Oceania.

Although the Taiping Rebellion began as a religious and moral movement against the hated Manchu barbarians, it quickly turned violent, destroying shrines and temples and vanquishing imperial troops. An estimated 20 million people, most of them noncombatants, died in the religious and political conflict. The Ghost Dance Movement, which swept from west to east across the northern plains of the United States and Canada, also began as a religious and moral movement. Native Americans expected to see the resurrection of their ancestors, the return of the buffalo, and the vanishing of the whites. Ethical conduct rather than warfare would effect this transformation. But on 29 December 1890, the Seventh Cavalry – the survivors of General Custer's failed last stand – surrounded a small band of Lakota Sioux at a creek called Wounded Knee and killed 150 Native Americans, more than half of whom were women and children. The Wounded Knee Massacre effectively ended the pan-Indian millennial movement. Finally, cargo cults were religious enterprises that developed in the islands of Melanesia, for the most part, in which indigenous peoples engaged in diverse actions – dancing ecstatically, burning seeds, destroying food stores, taking up arms – in expectation of an imminent day of plenty: the cargo that the Europeans enjoyed, brought on ships and planes, would soon be theirs. Some of the cargo cults had military or nationalist objectives, while others seemed purely religious. All, apparently, had millennial overtones.

Two additional historical cases should be mentioned, since they came to be compared with the mass deaths in Jonestown. In 73 CE, Jewish Zealots slew their wives and children before killing themselves when they saw that the Roman army was about to breach their hilltop fortress at Masada. Historical sources claim that 960 Jews died there, though remains of fewer than 30 bodies have been found. In the seventeenth and eighteenth centuries, the Russian Old Believers voluntarily submitted to martyrdom to protest liturgical changes in the Orthodox Church. An estimated 20,000 Old Believers died by immolating themselves and their captives when the tsar's forces attacked them. Had either group not faced imminent threats of persecution, torture, and death, it seems unlikely that they would have turned to self-inflicted violence. Yet apocalyptic worldviews had already led the Zealots into guerilla warfare against both the Romans and the Jewish collaborators, while an apocalyptic mood prompted a number of Old Believers to seek death even before their mass suicides (Robbins 1989b). In short, millennial expectations played a role in these antecedents as well.

Theories regarding crisis cults and messianic movements could have predicted responses to the far-reaching disruptions of the postwar period – the nationalist wars of independence, the Cold War, the coups and counter-coups fomented by political-corporate entities. Savior figures surfaced in developing nations, radical dualism materialized between what was known as the Free World and the Communist bloc, and a messianic complex for saving the world flourished in the United States. The effects of radical social change upon religious movements, as described by anthropologists and historians, can be observed in our own day.

4   Cults before Jonestown: The 1960s and 1970s

To understand the context for theoretical considerations of cult violence, we must first look at the entrance of NRMs and minority religions into the West and the attitudes ordinary people and scholars held about them. New spiritual alternatives – the Swedenborgian Church, Rosicrucianism, Neo-Templar and Martinist orders, Wicca – were born in Europe and contributed to post-Enlightenment religious freedom there (Melton 2002). After Indian Independence and the Chinese Revolution in the twentieth century, immigrants brought Asian beliefs and practices to the lands of their former colonial occupiers. Following the repeal of the Asian Exclusion Act in 1965 in the United States, an influx of gurus and roshis spawned interest in Asian religions.

This turn to the East had already begun in the 1950s, when those in the Beat Culture appropriated Zen Buddhism and its concept of emptiness (shunyata). The cool nihilism of jazz and the Beat Culture was replaced by hot Hinduism: incense, colorful clothing, ragas and sitars, ecstatic dancing, chanting. The Jesus Freaks made traditional Christianity hip, ecstatic, and spirit-filled. Ritual and practice replaced the dispassion of Zen and the formalism of mainline American religions. Moreover, the use of psychoactive drugs accompanied the experiential aspects of these new types of religion.

A call to commitment attended the budding political, social, and religious movements. One undertook the task to change the world, or oneself, as a serious endeavor requiring perseverance, zeal, and dedication. Perhaps most disturbing to those in the West was the emphasis found in these movements on communal, or community, well-being rather than individual fulfillment and gratification. Bellah saw the erosion of "individual utilitarianism" in many movements and interpreted "the crisis of the sixties above all as a crisis of meaning, a religious crisis, with major political, social, and cultural consequences" (Bellah 1976, 339). Idealistic young adults joined various antiwar, anticolonial, and antipoverty causes, and sought various religious practices – meditative, collective, pacifist – in order to make a difference. In this, they heeded their parents' call to make something of themselves, many times by joining new religions.

The "spiritual revolution" (Needleman 1970), or "new religious consciousness" (Glock and Bellah 1976), or "consciousness revolution" (Wuthnow 1976) could hardly escape notice, by either families or academics. While scholars studied the tremendous changes unfolding before their eyes with interest, parents viewed the rise of religious alternatives with anxiety. The word "cult," once rarely used and rather obscure, assumed sinister and dangerous connotations. A number of styles of cult watching developed as a result.

It is worth discussing the five cult-watching groups Barker (2002) identified so as to utilize value-neutral terminology. Once called the Anticult Movement (ACM), Cult Awareness Groups (CAGs) look at how NRMs may harm individuals or society; they are concerned about cult activities. Cult awareness scholars today see themselves as members of a Cult Awareness Movement, or CAM (Giambalvo, Kropveld, and Langone, n.d.), and this more euphonious term will be used rather than CAG. In contrast, countercult groups (CCGs) are concerned about cult beliefs and tend to be constituted of Christians who see heresy, heterodoxy, and unbelief to be the chief perils of NRMs. Research-Oriented Groups (ROGs), called Cult Apologists or Pro-Cultists by those in the CAM, examine the ways in which NRMs interact with society, contextualizing them in historical, sociological, or anthropological perspectives. The last two groups in Barker's typology – Human Rights Groups and Cult-Defender Groups – are concerned with the legal and civil rights of NRMs and their members.

This book differentiates between CAM and ROG studies in order to highlight the two main trajectories of investigations into violence and NRMs.

When we study the phenomenon of cult violence from a psychological angle, we tend to enter the realm of CAM research, especially as represented by scholars who write for the *International Journal of Cultic Studies* (formerly *Cultic Studies Review*) or *ISCA Today*. The treatment of violence in popular literature and the media also tends to be written from either the CAM standpoint or the CCG outlook. When we approach it from the historical or sociological direction, we are adopting a ROG perspective, which is the primary, though not the only, position presented in this book.

ROG reports throughout the 1960s and 1970s focused on the phenomenon of the expansion of new religions by young adults in the counterculture, though millennial groups, both historical and modern, also received attention. The topic of violence, however, rarely came up in either sociological or religious studies analyses (e.g., monographs lacking any mention of violence include Needleman 1970; Ellwood 1973; Glock and Bellah 1976; Wuthnow 1976). What did emerge were some themes that eventually gained importance, once religious violence became the object of inquiry in its own right.

The problem of radical dualism, for example, appeared in several studies. Roy's consideration of the "Communist Left and the Radical Right" asserted that fundamentalists believe that "the world is a battlefield and there are two contestants. One is God, who leads the legions of good. The other is Satan, who will face ultimate defeat but who will meanwhile gain major victories" (Roy 1964, 66). Anthony and Robbins observed that dualistic religions "tend to affirm the contrast between concrete exemplars of good and evil as a metaphysical principle" (Anthony and Robbins 1978, 93; see also Anthony and Robbins 1997). This dualistic contrast made Western religions in general, and Christianity in particular, "prone to ethnocentric and chauvinistic idolatries" (95). Wilson's (1970) sociological examination of sects also described the exclusivity and "us versus them" attitude typifying sectarian thinking. His typology of revolutionist sects (in which a divine or supernatural action will transform the world) and utopianist sects (in which humans themselves must remake society) suggested innately dualistic world-views that might, on occasion, justify outbreaks of violence – and which, historically speaking, did lead to bloodshed, such as that effected by the English revolutionists known as the Fifth Monarchy Men in the seventeenth century.

Another theme raised at this time, to be reprised in subsequent decades, was what Wallis (1975) called "epistemological authoritarianism" – that is, an unyielding dogmatism in which the group sees itself as presenting the only path to truth and salvation. Like Wilson, Wallis argued that sectarian groups are exclusive, offering "some unique and privileged means of access to the truth or salvation" (Wallis 1975, 9). Epistemological authoritarianism might inevitably produce the dogmatism, absolutism, fundamentalism, or theological dualism that might condone group violence, but this was not yet the concern of Wallis or the contributors to his 1975 collection of essays.

Yet a third theme in NRM studies that began to appear was the role played by a charismatic leader. Barkun (1974) saw the prophet figure as one of the essential elements in violent millennial movements. "The prophet is a synthesizer who takes ideas that already have currency and shapes them to meet the exigencies of social and cultural crisis" (Barkun 1974, 181). But leadership is a dyadic process: the messiah's charisma must be recognized by the disciples. "Charisma is not something one possesses, but rather shorthand for extraordinary qualities which followers impute" (88).

A final theme that gained traction later on concerned the repression of religious freedom and the violence directed against adherents of new religions. Cox's (1978) survey of the history of mainstream attacks on marginal religions exposed four recurrent myths in the CAM literature: the subversion myth (cultists are destabilizing society), the myth of sexual and behavioral deviancy (cultists are deviant), the myth of dissimulation (cultists all lie), and the myth of the evil eye (cultists have been brainwashed). Scholars presented historical occurrences of violence against Mormons, Catholics, and fringe Christians as evidence of an underground pattern of repression of apparent religious deviance (Cox 1978; Scheflin and Opton 1978). Still other academics characterized deprogramming as "the new exorcism" and asserted that it was a form of violence that involved physical, emotional, and verbal abuse that violated religious liberty (Shupe, Spielmann, and Stigall 1978).

Radical dualism, epistemological authoritarianism, charismatic leadership, and anticult violence, then, were some of the themes scholars introduced in this period that would be further developed after Jonestown. None of the research-oriented cult watchers seemed to anticipate violence; nor did they see the potential for danger. On the contrary, curiosity and a desire to understand these groups and to interpret them to outsiders marked their studies.

Countercult groups with a Christian orientation were undoubtedly the first of any cult-watching bodies to sound the alarm about the new religions. Their objections were theological, unrelated to any concern about violence other than that done to believers' souls. The classic work on the subject, *The Kingdom of the Cults* (Martin 1965), republished many times, included a range of groups identified as cults, from Christian Science and New Thought, to Jehovah's Witnesses and Mormons, to Father Divine's Peace Mission and the Nation of Islam. While Martin found an Orwellian aspect to the rise of cults, with their authoritarian pronouncements and their attempts to isolate members, he did not raise the specter of violence. Ironically, he expressed admiration for the missionary efforts that cultists made, though of course was critical of those who preyed on converts after major Christian evangelistic campaigns.

Approaching religion from their own vantage, journalists were constructing public opinion about "strange sects and curious cults" – the actual title of a book – in which sex (Bach 1961) and violence (Larsen 1971) dominated consideration of new religions. Whereas those writing from the ROG perspective directed arguments at their scholarly peers, reporters were aiming for a popular audience. Journalistic teams wrote two of the most influential books coming from the CAM standpoint: *All Gods' Children* (Stoner and Parke 1977) and *Snapping* (Conway and Siegelman 1978). Though neither work could come up with actual instances of cult violence, Conway and Siegelman mentioned Charles Manson, the Son of Sam, and Patty Hearst and the Symbionese Liberation Army as evidence of the violent proclivities inherent in cults. Stoner and Parke implied that members of the Children of God may have killed a reporter in Thailand and that Church of Scientology members may have had something to do with the "unexplained deaths" of two reporters writing a story about the group. They also quoted an elder in the Love Israel Family as saying that "it might one day be necessary to kill someone for disciplinary reasons" (Stoner and Parke 1977, 179). Most of the violence these journalists described was perpetrated within the group as brainwashing, sleep deprivation, malnutrition, and cult rituals and practices that "are psychologically unwholesome, and in some cases physically dangerous when they involve the use of drugs or perverse sexual rites" (Stoner and Parke 1977, 29).

It took another journalist, Tom Dulack, the ghostwriter for Ted Patrick's *Let Our Children Go!* (Patrick 1976) to explicitly prophesy violence. Patrick's fascinating apologia for deprogramming – which included kidnapping, confinement, restraint, and other illegal measures used to rescue adult children from cults – justified the process on the grounds that cult members had already lost free will through brainwashing. Twice Patrick declared that "[s]ome adherents believe they have a divine sanction to kill when necessary. I believe that in Hare Krishna you have essentially another Charles Manson movement – only many thousands of members strong" (Patrick 1976, 118). He maintained that members of the Unification Church were also willing to go against what their parents had taught them, even to murder. Patrick quoted the extended statement of a deprogrammed Moonie who had written,

"You might be told to sacrifice yourself, or to kill people, even those once close to you" (247).

While Patrick was correct in predicting a violent eruption, he was completely wrong about its source. Unification Church, ISKCON, Divine Light Mission, Children of God, and Scientology comprised the groups that alarmed parents in the 1960s and 1970s. Peoples Temple never sounded in any of these tocsins. "Prior to 1978, the Temple was not to be found featured in the anticult literature" (Barker 1986, 330).

5   After Jonestown: The 1980s

The study of New Religious Movements and collective violence – that is, murder and suicide committed for ideological reasons – can be said to begin with the deaths that occurred at an agricultural commune located in South America. In 1978, members of Peoples Temple, a religious movement based in California, committed mass murders and suicides at their utopianist community in Jonestown, which had been constructed in the jungles of the Northwest District of Guyana near the Venezuelan border. The violence was directed at both outsiders and insiders, beginning with the assassination of a United States congressman and three reporters who were investigating conditions in Jonestown at the request of concerned family members. It concluded with the murders and suicides of more than 900 men, women, and children through the ingestion of poison made with a fruit punch, an event that gave rise to the expression "drinking the Kool-Aid." A theology of revolutionary suicide – a belief in the redemptive power of martyrdom to achieve social change – seemed to fuel the events, although the exact nature of the deaths remains in dispute.

The bare particulars of the tragedy revealed how different Peoples Temple was from other new religions (Bromley and Shupe 1981; Richardson

1982; Bromley and Shupe 1989). The church was multiracial, with a majority of African American members, and had a large number of children and senior citizens. Its members worked from a progressive political stance and offered programs for those in poverty. Although it began as a Pentecostal church and later joined the Disciples of Christ denomination, Peoples Temple ultimately became a nonreligious intentional community. What it did share with other NRMs was a charismatic leader, an apocalyptic worldview, a dualistic outlook, and millennial hopes. Jim Jones (1931–1978), who cofounded the movement with his wife, Marceline Baldwin Jones (1927–1978), repeatedly invoked two specters of the age. The first was nuclear holocaust, which Jones described as imminent and inevitable throughout the Temple's twenty-five year history. The second was the institutional racism of American society, which would lead to the incarceration of minorities in concentration camps. The group believed that a number of forces, both individual and governmental, were conspiring against its very survival. This augmented members' belief in the righteousness of their own cause and the evil of those opposed to their aims. Yet successive moves – from Indiana to California, and from California to Guyana – indicated a millennial hope that the community might prevail if it found a homeland sufficiently removed from its enemies. With that hope seemingly dashed by the arrival of the congressional party, the group turned to murder and suicide, which they had been rehearsing both rhetorically and sacramentally for more than a year.

Despite the important differences it had from other cults, Peoples Temple and the deaths in Jonestown seemed to confirm the dire predictions the CAM had made and to prove that all new religions had malevolent proclivities. "The unprecedented media exposure given Jonestown has alerted Americans to the fact that seemingly beneficent religious groups can mask a hellish rot," began *The Lure of the Cults* (Enroth 1979, 13). Other CAM specialists opened their books and articles with passing references to

Jonestown, suggesting implicitly or declaring explicitly that all new religions had this lethal possibility (Rudin and Rudin 1980; Wooden 1981; Pavlos 1982; Appel 1983; Rudin 1984; Markowitz and Halperin 1984). Indeed, the argument *reductio ad Hitlerum* became a popular trope (Enroth 1979; Appel 1983; McConnell 1984). West summarized the consensus when he wrote that "most [cults] – if not all – have the potentiality of becoming deadly, as the Temple of Jim Jones did" (West 1990, 20). In these essentialist analyses, the deaths in Jonestown demonstrated that violence is inherent in all NRMs, regardless of environment, ideology, demography, or other factors.

In the wake of the tragedy, the CAM received a forum for shaping public opinion about new religions. It gave anticultists wide access to the news media and government agencies. "Jonestown both objectified the anticultists' own worst fears about the destructive potential of cults and provided a concrete referent to which they could point as evidence in their appeals to the public and to political officials" (Shupe and Bromley 1980, 114). Critics of the CAM went further and claimed that new religions were the victims, rather than the perpetrators, of violence. Kidnapping and deprogramming of NRM members was the real danger the "new vigilantes" posed by practicing a militant form of "bigotry" (Shupe and Bromley 1980; Bromley and Shupe 1981; Melton and Moore 1982).

Quickie paperbacks and first-person narratives about Peoples Temple shared the cult awareness perspective, primarily because most sources, though not all, were apostates – that is, former members who publicly criticized the group. Reporters relied upon members of the Concerned Relatives – an oppositional group comprised of former members and families – for deciphering Temple beliefs and practices (e.g., Kilduff and Javers 1978; Krause 1978). A notable exception to these books was *Raven* (Reiterman and Jacobs 1982), a well-researched journalistic account, although it started from the premise that Jim Jones was insane from early childhood. Countercult analyses believed that the

Temple's non-biblical, or even anti-biblical, stance was the reason behind its violent end (e.g., Kerns 1979; Thielmann 1979), and some even saw the hand of Satan (White 1979).

In the decade following Jonestown, mental health assessments of both leaders and followers developed to explain incidents of religious violence. Many psychologists and psychiatrists conjectured that "a leader's mental disturbance can play an important role in the emergence of violent behavior in a charismatic group" (Galanter 1989, 192; see also Lasaga 1980). Others concluded that individuals with "identity dislocation" or problematic self-concepts turned to new religions, and violence, to resolve personal problems – to put it rather simplistically (Zurcher 1982; Deutsch 1989). Still others noted a codependent relationship between leaders and followers that amplified the deviance already present in the group (Johnson 1979; Mills 1982; A. Smith 1982; Ulman and Abse 1983; Weightman 1984; Stark and Bainbridge 1985; Robbins 1988; Jones 1989). While these analyses seemed to differ, in reality they all accentuated internal cult dynamics rather than interactions between NRMs and outsiders. Moreover, they tended to attribute violence to the derangement of the leader, who either persuaded, conditioned, or coerced followers to commit unspeakable acts for irrational reasons.

Although scholars of sociology and religious studies published a number of articles evaluating the violence that occurred in Jonestown (for extensive bibliographies, see Lindt 1981–82; Robbins 1989a; Moore 2016), and cult controversies in general (Beckford 1985; Barker 1986), only four scholarly books focused on Jonestown in the ten years after 1978. Ken Levi's *Violence and Religious Commitment* (Levi 1982b) brought together a dozen academic essays, with several papers providing a comparative perspective on "sect violence." Levi himself argued that violence was the effect of extreme group cohesion and asserted that most violence would probably occur in "authoritarian totalistic sects," especially those in which homicide or suicide was believed to be a means to "sectarian ends" (Levi 1982a, 7). Hall described the paradoxical nature of Peoples Temple as both a this-worldly and other-worldly apocalyptic sect: when opponents thwarted the ambitions of the worldly sect, Jones transferred the goals to an afterlife, so that revolutionary suicide, "in contrast to revolution itself, is a victory" (Hall 1982, 54).

The essays in Levi's collection took different positions on the issue of violence. While Hall (1982) saw a dynamic interplay between Temple members and their enemies, Mills (1982) attributed the group's demise to a reduction of normative dissonance in which violence was legitimated; in his view, Jim Jones' growing paranoia influenced his inner circle, which in turn uncritically accepted their leader's every dictate. This "super-commitment" provided a standard for the entire group, thus setting the stage for violence. Similarly, Redlinger and Armour (1982) claimed that neophytes to cults were resocialized to become psychologically dependent upon the group, taking their behavioral cues from role models for the new reality. By fabricating the past and reinterpreting the present, NRMs could defend the use of violence.

Weightman (1984) also examined the process of resocialization in her monograph on Jonestown. Rejecting psychologized explanations of pathology, deviance, brainwashing, and mental illness, she argued instead for the existence of a socially constructed reality in which a nonnormative discourse − by society's standards − isolated group members in their valorization of laying down their lives for the group (i.e., committing suicide). In her eyes, Jones created a "highly polemical reality" that contrasted socialism (Jonestown) against fascism (U.S. society) (Weightman 1984, 152). Weightman posited that adults, along with their children − many of whom had grown up in the Temple − adopted Jones' discourse, and his authority, as their own. It was not brainwashing but rather socialization that led to the mass murder-suicides.

Chidester's "religiohistorical interpretation" of Peoples Temple and Jonestown assigned violence to an ideology in which social immorality was symbolized "as an absorption into the transcendent, timeless moment of the socialist revolution" (Chidester 1988, 125). Revolutionary suicide functioned as a loyalty test and as a way to avoid a dehumanizing death. Although Chidester noted the impact of oppositional forces – relatives, the news media, and government agencies – he concluded that "collective suicide was imagined as the ultimate *revolutionary* act, in the sense that it would radically invert the entire systematic classification of persons in which the members of Peoples Temple had experienced themselves as subclassified" (Chidester 1988, 159). Like Weightman and others, Chidester advanced an explanation that looked to internal factors, rather than to external interrelationships, as the root cause of the deaths in Jonestown.

In contrast, Hall (1987) blamed the deaths in part on the cultural opponents of Jim Jones who sought to dismantle Jonestown. Regardless of Jones' megalomania, "it is no longer possible to understand People Temple apart from the actions of its detractors" (Hall 1987, 289). For Hall, the key to understanding religious violence was to identify recurring elements in the conflicts between religious communities and political orders. In the case of Jonestown, "without a decisive showdown with forsworn opponents . . . it is much less likely that the deaths would have occurred" (Hall 1987, 295). Though not the first proponent (see J. Smith 1982; Moore 1985), Hall was most certainly the strongest advocate of what would later be called the interactionist theory of violence.

Thus, analyses of the violence at Jonestown ranged from imputing the actions to the (probably insane) charismatic leader and his brainwashed, or emotionally disturbed, followers; to arguing that an ideology of violence inherent to the group was at play; to claiming that external forces bore some responsibility for what was happening within the group. But after an initial flurry of publications about Jonestown, interest in cult violence dropped off among research-oriented scholars. Instead, the subject of religious extremism, or radical religion, dominated the literature. Furthermore, studies of prophetic religions, apocalypticism, millennialism, and "fundamentalisms" attempted to illuminate the rise of Islam, Islamism, and other political activism in the name of religion (e.g., Esposito 1983; Hyman 1985; Hadden and Shupe 1986; Saiedi 1986; Daniels 1992; Marty and Appleby 1993).

Those involved in the CAM, especially reporters and law enforcement officials, were more concerned about supposed satanic and occult practices than about religious extremism in the 1980s. A moral panic resulted, in which accusations of molestation of children in childcare centers sent many adults to prison, and recovered memory syndrome fed tabloid and television hunger for the sensational (Richardson, Best, and Bromley 1991). The index to Saliba's bibliography on *Social Science and the Cults* (1990) displayed the high anxiety over occultic mayhem: entries for the occult (60) and those for witchcraft (30) and Satanism (17) outnumbered those for "violence and the cults" (11) and even charismatic leadership (19).

It seems disrespectful of the dead to say so, but the 918 fatalities in Jonestown were insufficient to sustain extended treatments of cult violence. And then Waco happened – and subsequently the Solar Temple, Aum Shinrikyō, Heaven's Gate, and the Movement for the Restoration of the Ten Commandments of God. These were the events that put violence and NRMs back into public awareness.

6 After Waco: The 1990s

On 28 February 1993, an attempt by the U.S. Bureau of Alcohol, Tobacco, and Firearms (ATF) to serve a search warrant for weapons led to a firefight between federal agents and members of a small religious community. Four agents and six civilians died that day, while twenty agents and four civilians were also wounded (Wessinger 2000a). The Branch Davidians, an offshoot of the Seventh-day Adventist Church, had established a community called Mount Carmel outside Waco, Texas. About 130 men, women, and children lived communally under the inspiration of their charismatic leader, David Koresh (1959–1993), whose biblical exegesis unlocked the secrets of the book of Revelation, according to survivors. It was undeniable that the Branch Davidians were engaged in buying and selling weapons at gun shows to raise revenue and to prepare for what they believed was the looming battle of Armageddon. It was also undeniable that the search warrant could have been served peacefully, without the show of force the ATF had planned. After the botched raid, the U.S. Federal Bureau of Investigation (FBI) took over management of the tense situation.

Over a fifty-one day period, FBI negotiators spoke with Davidians inside their complex, attempting to mediate a peaceful surrender; meanwhile, the agency's Hostage Rescue Team, in charge of tactical operations, exhibited a show of force designed to coerce the group into submission. Because the FBI considered Koresh to be a con man who used religion to bend reluctant followers to his will, agents did not see the standoff as a religious event – that is, one in which religious beliefs and values were at stake. They did not consult with religious studies scholars, apart from a church historian from nearby Baylor University, and they called Koresh's interpretive discussions "Bible babble" (Wessinger 2000a, 74). Two biblical studies scholars saw it differently, however. Philip Arnold of the Reunion Institute in Houston, Texas, and James Tabor of the University of North Carolina, Charlotte, traveled to Waco and discussed the Bible with Koresh via local talk radio. Arnold and Tabor were, and remain, convinced that their conversations opened up the possibility of a nonviolent end to the confrontation through a reinterpretation of scripture. Koresh told the FBI that he would surrender at the end of Passover, which the Branch Davidians observed, once he had finished writing a commentary on the seventh seal in the book of Revelation.

But on 19 April, U.S. Attorney General Janet Reno authorized a gas attack on the community, with the idea that Branch Davidian adults would come out peacefully and that the children living with them would be saved. Beginning at 6:00 a.m., Bradley armored tanks punched holes in the residences, demolishing walls in order to insert CS gas; at least two potentially incendiary rounds were utilized. A fire started at noon and quickly spread, destroying what was left of the buildings. Nine Branch Davidians escaped, but seventy-six died, including seven teenagers and twenty-two children, among them two infants who were born during the gas assault (Wessinger 2016). Although the question of how exactly the fire started is controversial, the consensus seems to be that the Branch Davidians used accelerants to ignite the blaze. A consensus also exists, however, that no fire would have been contemplated had not the FBI launched the gas attack.

At least two sharp distinctions stood between the mass deaths in Jonestown and those in Waco. First, the Branch Davidians were in a situation of clear and present danger that anyone could observe, unlike Peoples Temple members, where the jeopardy, though real to the community, did not seem so ruinous. Second, though the Branch Davidians expected to fight the battle of Armageddon, they did not have a theology of revolutionary suicide; rather, they believed in armed struggle against the forces of Antichrist arrayed in Israel, as the Bible foretold. Jonestown residents, in contrast, believed that their sacrificial deaths would not only protest capitalism and the conditions of an inhumane world, but also demonstrate the righteousness of their cause.

The prominent role of control agents in precipitating the entire Branch Davidian crisis led the U.S. Department of Justice and the FBI to immediately investigate the actions federal officials took. Two studies undertaken by the FBI itself noted the contradictory advice given and the conflicting actions taken throughout the standoff (Dennis 1993; Report 1993). In addition to these and other self-studies, the FBI commissioned a group of attorneys, physicians, law enforcement officials, and religious studies scholars to produce an independent review. These latter investigators remarked on the FBI's failure to consider the religious worldviews of the Davidians in constructing an "alternative symbolic world" (Ammerman 1993, n.p.).

On the second anniversary of the final assault, Timothy McVeigh, a self-styled radical militiaman, blew up a federal building in Oklahoma City, Oklahoma, killing 168 and injuring more than 680 others as a protest of federal actions in Waco. This in turn led to a congressional investigation into the activities of federal law enforcement agencies at Waco, with highly publicized hearings in 1996. The congressional report, as well as other analyses, particularly pointed out the problematic nature of the intelligence that agents received from anticult experts and former members (Ammerman 1993; Tabor and Gallagher 1995; *Materials* 1997). The report contained internal FBI documents that revealed federal agency missteps. The Justice Department commissioned yet another study of Waco in 1999, appointing former U.S. senator John Danforth as a special counsel to investigate the FBI's use of force on the final day. A year later, the "Danforth Report" largely exonerated federal officials of any wrongdoing.

This was not the case with scholarly appraisals of the events from the research-oriented perspective, and condemnation of what happened at Mount Carmel was swift (Lewis 1994; Wright 1995b; Tabor and Gallagher 1995). The significant part played by oppositional groups – apostates, the news media, and anticult groups – in defining both Koresh and the Branch Davidians shaped government perception of them and its response at Waco (Wright 1995a). Opponents used the threat of mass suicide as a theme symbolizing the menace of all cults. According to Hall (1995), they constructed a "genetic bridge" between Jonestown and the Branch Davidians in which two unrelated groups became connected through oppositional rhetoric. Scholars also criticized the role of the news media in fabricating a narrative of good versus evil that served to demonize the Branch Davidians and justify actions taken against them (Richardson 1995; Shupe and Hadden 1995). Finally, the fact that the religious worldviews of the Davidians were ignored had toxic repercussions.

> The widespread failure to take the religious convictions of Koresh and the other Davidians seriously, signaled by the facile adoption of the term "cult," contributed directly to their deaths. ... Since "cults" represent a dangerous threat to the social order, it is necessary to oppose them with all the resources that the state can muster, including tear gas, SWAT teams, and tanks (Tabor and Gallagher 1995, 118).

Waco gave scholars both the opportunity and the data to think about cult violence comparatively. While generalizations had been made after Jonestown, a second case study undermined some assumptions. Robbins and Anthony (1995) singled out two factors contributing to the possibility of violence occurring within new religious movements: exogenous elements, which relate to hostility, stigmatization, and persecution experienced at the hands of outsiders; and endogenous elements, which are properties belonging to the movement itself, such as leadership, beliefs, rituals, and organization. The authors concluded that endogenous factors in the case of Jonestown – such as the group's apocalyptic beliefs, charismatic leadership, and communal boundary tension – played a greater role in the outcome than did the endogenous considerations at Mount Carmel. In other words, exogenous factors such as anticult opposition, hostile media coverage, and aggressive state actions contributed to, or even created, the events at Waco.

Those in the Cult Awareness Movement saw things differently. The president and the director of the American Family Foundation (AFF – renamed International Cultic Studies Association in 2004) made a joint statement the day after the climax, proclaiming that "Cults are massive, enduring cons. . . . All cult leaders are charismatic, persuasive personalities. Those that are at the top of their trade gain virtually absolute control over their followers" (quoted in Bardin 1994). These AFF officials did not fault the FBI for the outcome, instead assigning Koresh "ultimate responsibility" and asserting that the result was perhaps inevitable. Margaret Singer and Herbert Rosedale (quoted in Bardin 1994) also disputed religious studies scholar Nancy Ammerman's claim in her report to the FBI that "the notion of 'cult brainwashing' has been thoroughly discredited in the academic community" (Ammerman 1993, n.p.).

Ammerman was correct, however, in pointing out that research-oriented scholars had dismissed brainwashing – also called coercive persuasion, mind control, or "pathogenic mental conditioning" (Robbins 1988, 188) – as an explanatory factor for either NRM conversion or violence (e.g., Barker 1984; Beckford 1985; Bromley and Shupe 1989). Margaret Singer, the most public champion for theories of brainwashing, had earlier come under attack in academic journals and in the courts (Richardson 1985; Melton 1999). By the twenty-first century, even those in the CAM were reformulating the concept of brainwashing "into a more nuanced analysis of mind manipulation and totalistic milieu dynamics" (Rudin 2002, n.p.), going so far as to call it, instead, "unethical social influence" (Giambalvo, Kropveld, and Langone n.d.). This change in the CAM resulted in a repudiation of deprogramming efforts in the 1990s, since deprogramming presupposed an initial involuntary programming.

Scholars writing in *Cultic Studies Journal* after 1993 juxtaposed Waco and Jonestown as more or less similar events that demonstrated the ongoing hazards of unscrupulous leaders exerting mind control. "For me," wrote Singer, "Waco was a replay of Jonestown" (Singer and Lalich 1995, 28). Galanter (1999) assumed that the Branch Davidians planned to commit mass suicide and asked how they came to make that decision. He answered his own question by attributing the deaths to the manipulations of David Koresh, who wanted to maintain "absolute control" of his flock. Galanter went on to list the (primarily endogenous) qualities that led a group to violence. In sum, it was evident that CAM analyses focused on endogenous factors – to the exclusion of any other considerations – to explain cult violence.

Waco seemed to be just the first in a series of murderous encounters involving new religions that occurred between 1993 and the year 2000. Three comprehensive evaluations from the research-oriented perspective published at the turn of the millennium warrant notice before discussing the incidents. These studies generated theories that were tested against actual historical events and served as the backdrop against which later arguments were made. They compared not only the events of Jonestown and Waco, but also examined four specific cases: three instances of murder-suicides committed by members of the Order of the Solar Temple in France, Switzerland, and Quebec, Canada, in 1994, 1995, and 1997; the subway gas attack in Tokyo perpetrated by followers of Aum Shinrikyō in 1995; the suicides of adherents of Heaven's Gate in San Diego, California, in 1997; and the murder-suicides of the Movement for the Restoration of the Ten Commandments of God that took place in Uganda in 2000.

Apocalypse Observed (Hall, Schuyler, and Trinh 2000) propelled the interactionist theory first suggested by Hall (1987) in his analysis of Jonestown. The authors articulated a pattern of conflict to explain that "religious violence [is] a product of the *interaction* between a broadly apocalyptic religious movement and opponents in the outside world who are contesting whether the movement has the cultural legitimacy to pursue its collective vision" (Hall et al. 2000, 11, italics in original). If opponents successfully persuade the media and governments that the group is a threat, then the group rightly perceives the opposition as threatening. The authors explicitly rejected endogenous explanations of events in Jonestown, Waco, Tokyo, and in the Solar Temple, arguing that "the extreme violence unleashed by these groups did not arise solely on the basis of dynamics internal to the groups themselves" (12).

How the Millennium Comes Violently further elaborated the typology Wessinger introduced in a prior article (Wessinger 1997; Wessinger 2000a). Bypassing the confusion caused by terms like "premillennialism" and "post-millennialism" – which refer specifically to Christian theological expectations – Wessinger constructed two categories to encompass any religion holding millennial beliefs. *Catastrophic millennialism* "involves a pessimistic view of humanity and society" in which the millennial kingdom will occur "only after the violent destruction of the old world." In contrast, *progressive millennialism* has an optimistic view in which "humans engaging in social work in harmony with the divine will can effect changes that non-catastrophically and progressively create the millennial kingdom" (Wessinger 2000a, 16–17). The author further explained how catastrophic or progressive millennial groups may embrace violence if they are (1) fragile (that is, experiencing internal weakness and external cultural opposition); (2) assaulted (that is, facing attack by state actors because the group is perceived to be dangerous); or (3) revolutionary (that is, having an ideology that justifies violence to achieve the millennial goals). Blending interactionist with exogenous-endogenous explanations to create a continuum of possibilities, she applied these typologies in analyses of groups that had violent endings (Jonestown, Waco, Aum Shinrikyō, Solar Temple, and Heaven's Gate) and those that did not (the Montana Freemen and the Chen Tao group).

Finally, the articles in *Cults, Religion and Violence* (Bromley and Melton 2002b) presented sociological explanations for "dramatic denouements" – namely, "[climactic] moments during which a final project of ultimate moral reckoning is undertaken [that] must be understood historically, processually, and interactively" (Bromley and Melton 2002a, 4). Focusing on Waco, Solar Temple, Aum Shinrikyō, and Heaven's Gate, but using additional events from past and present, the contributors showed that cult violence is actually an anomaly, contingent upon the interaction of competing parties. Bromley (2002) argued that most new religions exist in some sort of latent tension with the wider society and that this tension may blossom into a nascent conflict in which adversaries are acknowledged. As the rivalry escalates to intensified struggle, both parties see the other as dangerous. At the final reckoning, or dramatic denouement, violence explodes in order for the group to maintain its core identity – and even its very existence. "Heightened mobilization and radicalization of these movements, mobilization and radicalization of opposi-tional groups, and the entrance of third-party control agencies into the conflict" all serve to advance the process toward a bloody culmination (Bromley 2002, 20). According to Barker (2002), the unintended consequence of CAM cult watching may actually provoke violence against groups through the legitimiza-tion of verbal, legal, or physical attacks upon them. Finally, Robbins (2002) concentrated on specific internal variables that might contribute to violence, building upon the endogenous-exogenous argument he and Anthony intro-duced to examine the events in Waco (Robbins and Anthony 1995). He found that apocalyptic worldviews combined with a totalistic social structure in which group members are isolated and encapsulated can fuse together in a deadly way.

These three studies propounded many reasons for a handful of new religions resorting to violence against themselves and their perceived enemies. A look at the circumstances themselves shows why the events provoked such a range of theoretical explanations.

The Order of the Solar Temple (Ordre du Temple Solaire, or OTS) had its roots in Western esotericism, neo-Templarism, twentieth-century Rosicrucianism, and the New Age Movement (Bogdan 2011). Cofounded by Joseph Di Mambro (1924–1994), a professional swindler, and Luc Jouret (1947–1994), a homeopathic doctor, the group comprised individuals from the upper classes of Francophone Europe, Canada, and the Caribbean (Mayer 1999; Hall et al. 2000). In the late 1980s, discussions began within the OTS regarding "transit" to another planet to survive an impending environmental disaster, though suicide was not explicitly discussed at that time. Then in October 1994 police found the bodies of fifty-three people in several locations in Switzerland and Quebec; some had been murdered, some had committed suicide, and in a number of cases the choice for death was unclear because arson had destroyed evidence. In 1995, sixteen more people died in an apparent group suicide in France, their bodies set on fire by two remaining members, who then killed themselves. An additional five true believers died in Quebec in March 1997. "Outside of possible explanations linked to Di Mambro's mental state," wrote Mayer, "it seems likely that criticism by ex-members, episodic public exposure in Martinique and Québec, and disappointed hopes for success led the Solar Temple's leadership to revise their view of the future" (Mayer 1999, 182). Yet Mayer argued that internal dissent, along with the desire to make a mark on history – as evidenced by declarations sent to the media to coincide with publicity about the deaths – also served as factors in making the decision to die.

Introvigne and Mayer (2002) later appraised contradictory stories that arose to describe the OTS transits. French-speaking media used a narrative that relied upon anticult stereotypes and claimed that OTS followers had been brainwashed. Another media motif suggested that OTS was not really a religion but rather a front for a nefarious enterprise, such as the Mafia or a terrorist organization. NRM scholars developed a third narrative, which centered on the mental and physical decline of Joseph Di Mambro and his decision to annihilate the group before he died. A fourth narrative, familiar by now, was that external forces exacerbated internal tensions and figuratively ignited the fires that literally consumed the group. Introvigne and Mayer concluded by presenting the four factors that they felt rightly described the tragedy: "predisposing apocalyptic ideology, perception of external opposition, internal dissent and apostasy, and crumbling charismatic authority of the leader" (Introvigne and Mayer 2002, 178). The combination of these features, and no single element alone, was what caused the OTS murders and suicides.

Taking a different tack, Lewis (2005) situated his examination of OTS in the context of other suicidal groups – Peoples Temple and Heaven's Gate – rather than that of all violent groups. Arguing against both millennialist (Wessinger 2000a) and interactionist explanations (Hall et al. 2000), Lewis focused on the leaders themselves. He found that the heads of the three suicide cults shared an intolerance of dissenting views, a need for total commitment, and paranoia about external threats to the group. An additional common factor was the leader's belief in his own approaching death. "If the three suicide leaders all perceived themselves as dying, then the notion of bringing the whole group ... along on their postmortem journeys might strike them as attractive" (Lewis 2005, 310). A final shared element was the fact that each group was in decline, and no successor had been appointed to carry the group beyond the leader's death.

A more recent meta-analysis conducted by Bogdan (2011) criticized the proposals of Lewis, Wessinger, and Hall et al. as not sufficiently appreciating the unique characteristics of OTS. Bogdan introduced the theories of Åkerbäck (2008) to English-speaking readers: the Swedish historian of religions found that previous descriptions of millennial beliefs were too vague and general and that suicide cults had more differences than similarities. Åkerbäck classified the distinctive tenets of various groups into three ideologies: an ideology of opposition (Peoples Temple), a temporary ideology (Solar Temple), and an

Beyond Brainwashing

ideology of metamorphosis (Heaven's Gate). Bogdan's own thesis was that OTS members understood their deaths as a final ritual of purification undertaken to advance to a higher level of spiritual, rather than physical, existence.

If members of OTS sought to purify themselves by fire, adherents of Aum Shinrikyō sought to purify the world by fire. In destroying an evil and corrupt society riddled with materialism and perversion, the extremely ascetic followers of Aum would save it. Initially a syncretistic blend of Buddhism, Hinduism, yoga, and severe austerities, Aum adopted an increasingly apocalyptic mindset under its founder and leader ASAHARA Shōkō (b. 1955; following convention, the last name appears first in small capital letters). The blind guru argued that the world was polluted with absolute evil, was irredeemable, and thus was deserving of destruction. Although the first death that occurred within Aum was an accident – the result of extreme self-denial – the cover-up of the death compromised believers and paved the way for the murders of defectors and opponents – and ultimately the gas attack in March 1995. During rush hour, Aum followers released the deadly sarin gas on trains and at the Kasumigaseki subway station, located near government ministries and the national police headquarters. Thirteen people died, and thousands more were injured.

Like OTS, Aum Shinrikyō – which means Supreme Truth – attracted the well educated. Quite a few scientists and technocrats worked in Aum's state-of-the-art laboratories to develop weapons of mass destruction. Between 1990 and 1995, devotees of ASAHARA staged at least fourteen biological and chemical attacks in Japan (Lifton 1999); the group probably killed more people throughout its history than died in the single attack that brought it to international notoriety.

Lifton (1999) and Reader (2000) saw internal, rather than external, dynamics at play. (Reader's later work emphasized the responsibility of ASAHARA more than did his first book on the subject [Reader 1996]). An ideology of *poa*, in which murder was justified, "came to mean not simply an act of merit transfer after death but a practice of intercession beforehand in order to 'save' the unworthy by 'transforming' their spirits so they could enter a higher spiritual realm" (Reader 2000, 18–19). *Poa*, then, was a form of altruistic killing that would save someone's soul through the elimination of their bad karma. This theology of violence, a world-rejecting view of society, the group's access to weapons of mass destruction, and ASAHARA'S totalistic control over his followers had a momentum that swept Aum Shinrikyō into its plan to instigate Armageddon (Lifton 1999).

Rejecting the notion that endogenous ingredients such as apocalyptic doctrines or leader-follower relationships led to Aum's increasingly destructive behavior, Hall et al. argued that the movement's "distinctiveness lies in how its apocalyptic theology developed in relation to its conflicts with opponents, the media, and the state" (Hall et al. 2000, 107). Repp (2011) also took an interactionist approach, which appreciated both endogenous and exogenous components. He first described the internal elements by which Aum triggered violence, including control of its boundary, renunciation of society, and the youth of its members – all three of which tended to isolate the group. He then distinguished four external characteristics that served to provoke, or encourage, the group: the mass media's one-sided coverage, law enforcement negligence, the involvement of politicians, and the government's failure to control the trade of chemical agents. The incapacity of institutional actors to learn the religious worldview of Aum also facilitated the catastrophe. Repp summarized the nonreligious contributions to the disaster in this way: psychological (a youthful membership), social (a new community with weak boundaries), political (Aum's disappointment with not establishing a successful political party), institutional (sensationalistic media coverage coupled with neglect by public officials), and economic (Aum's moneymaking schemes). He then concluded that the term "religious violence" was inappropriate in connection with Aum

Shinrikyō, given that secular considerations were a greater influence on what occurred than were doctrinal reasons.

One occurrence of violence on which most theorists seemed to agree was that of Heaven's Gate, during which thirty-nine members of a UFO group committed suicide – or, in their words, graduated to The Level Above Human (TELAH). In March 1997, the San Diego Sheriff's Department found a mansion full of similarly attired individuals who had ingested a sedative and then methodically tied plastic bags over their heads with rubber bands, sealing them around their necks. The deaths occurred over a two-day period; two individuals placed identical purple shrouds over the face of each corpse before they then killed themselves. Members had recorded videos for relatives and the general public, saying good-bye and explaining what they were doing and why they were happy to be leaving earth.

While superficially similar to the Solar Temple in its well-educated demographic and in the belief in transit to another planet, Heaven's Gate had important differences. Members of the "class" – called Heaven's Gate by the media only after the deaths because of its website – believed that human life on earth was limited and lacking. Their earthly bodies were mere containers or vehicles to be disposed of as they moved to TELAH, a higher state of being. The peripatetic founders of the group – Bonnie Lu Nettles (1927–1985) and Marshall Applewhite (1931–1997), affectionately called Bo and Peep or Ti and Do (after the musical scale) – blended together Christian and New Age concepts in which self-transformation through the gradual denigration, and eventual destruction, of the human body would effect salvation (Zeller 2014). Strict asceticism regarding food, clothing, lifestyle, and especially sex governed the several dozen who lived and worked together in anticipation of a sign marking the time of ultimate transformation. That sign came with the comet Hale-Bopp, with its extremely long tail lighting up the sky for several months. Rather than turn away from the chance when it offered itself, the

Heaven's Gate class eagerly embraced the opportunity to advance spiritually (Hall et al. 2000).

Balch and Taylor (2002) argued that suicide was a rational response in the worldview of the group. They observed three general factors that would play a role in the decision to die: (1) the conditions predisposing the group to radical action, (2) situational factors influencing the group's assessment of options, and (3) "precipitating events that transformed suicide from an option to a reality" (Balch and Taylor 2002, 224). Suicide was the logical conclusion to Heaven's Gate's progressive and deliberate disconnection from society and from everything human, which included the body. Zeller (2011) agreed that a process of "euphemization of violence" occurred over a long period of time in which the rhetorical rejection of the body slowly grew to mean suicide. Although the group posted comments on the Internet about "laying down" their human bodies and that true suicide would be rejecting the offer of spiritual eternal life, neither the media, law enforcement, nor cult-watching groups took notice. The deaths of Heaven's Gate adherents did not come out of an apocalyptic mindset – though they did believe that the earth would be "spaded over" in the near future – but were "religious acts" (Zeller 2011) that affirmed their faith that they would be transported to another planet (Hall et al. 2000).

Wessinger (2000a) offered a different reason for the deaths when she claimed that the repeated frustration in gaining recruits and the failure of the anticipated flying saucers to pick up the class suggested the disintegration of the millennial goal of the group. Prompted by the actual death of Nettles in 1985 and the possibility of Applewhite's death, students in the class found leaving earth preferable to staying. Lewis (2005) also found a number of qualities of the leader, along with the lack of future growth or prospects, to be decisive in Heaven's Gate's final reckoning.

Although an increase in religious violence was anticipated leading up to the turn of the millennium, this did not happen. In a document titled *Project*

Megiddo, the FBI attempted to predict who might be involved in domestic terrorism due to millennial expectations. The agency's risk assessment named Christian Identity, white supremacist and militia groups, Black Hebrew Israelites, and "Apocalyptic Cults," though it failed to mention any Islamic groups (Federal Bureau of Investigation 1999). Drawing primarily from CAM and law enforcement sources, the discussion of religion tended to concentrate on the leader of the group – noting the leader's mental state, physical health, fantasies, and fears – and the length of time "the leader's behavior has gone unchecked against outside authority" (Federal Bureau of Investigation 1999, 27). Yet the FBI's Critical Incident Analysis Group, established in 1994 (a year after the Waco disaster), did attempt to maintain a dialogue with scholars between 1995 and 1999 who were part of the American Academy of Religion (AAR) and the Center for Studies on New Religions (CESNUR). In dialogue with FBI agents and consultants, these academics provided a counterweight to the anticult perspective, although they had not been consulted in the drafting of the *Project Meggido* report (Barkun 2002).

Project Megiddo differentiated between offensive and defensive violent tendencies, presenting the Branch Davidians and their attempt to protect their enclave from attack as an example of defensive violence. It also distinguished between groups that want to expedite the Endtime, such as Aum Shinrikyō, and those that wish to survive by withdrawing from the world. Finally, the report cited Gilmartin's "lethal triad" (Gilmartin 1996), which foretold the essential constituents for violence to occur: group isolation from the world; the projection of responsibility for decisions upon the leader and the projection of blame for all group grievances upon outsiders; and "pathological anger" at perceived enemies, which inflamed a sense of righteousness and justification (Federal Bureau of Investigation 1999).

Despite predictions by the FBI, CAM and ROG scholars, and others, however, the millennium turned from 1999 to 2000 without apparent incident. Then came the news of an apparent mass suicide in Uganda in March 2000.

The African nation had been the site of religiously inspired violence in the past and would be again in the twenty-first century. In the 1980s, a spirit named Lakwena, speaking through Alice Auma (1957?–2007), promised to free Ugandans from the witchcraft that controlled the land, self-evident in the brutal regimes of Idi Amin Dada (1923–2003), Milton Obote (1925–2005), and Yoweri Museveni (b. 1944). The Holy Spirit Movement, an NRM that mixed together indigenous and Christian ideas and practices, attracted a number of ethnic groups that sought a sinless government based in morality. Soldiers in the Holy Spirit Mobile Forces (HSMF) went through a lengthy purification rite that included burning pagan charms and being baptized. Alice Lakwena, who took her spirit guide's name, promulgated a list of "safety precautions" for members of the army that forbade killing enemy soldiers – including prisoners of war – declining to take cover during battles but singing hymns instead, and refusing to remove (or steal) any items left on the battlefield (Behrend 1999, 47). Because Lakwena protected them, soldiers marched into battle, naked to the waist, standing upright to face the enemy. They also utilized a medicinal oil that supposedly rendered the HSMF bullet-proof. As the troops began a two-year march toward Kampala, a number of surprising military victories against various factions, including the National Resistance Army (NRA) of Museveni, seemed to attest to Alice's miraculous powers. In the end, however, the NRA defeated the HSMF in 1987, and the spirit Lakwena departed from Alice.

Though Alice Lakwena died in a refugee camp, the infamous Joseph Kony (b. 1961), leader of the Lord's Resistance Army (LRA), took up the cause of rebellion. Kony and the LRA are known chiefly for the abduction and enslavement of more than 30,000 children over a thirty-year period. The LRA hoped to set up a government in Uganda based upon the biblical Ten

Commandments but was driven out of the country and, greatly weakened, operated out of the Democratic Republic of Congo, Sudan, and the Central African Republic. In May 2017, the governments of Uganda and the United States officially abandoned their search for Kony.

Sandwiched between Lakwena and Kony, the Movement for the Restoration of the Ten Commandments of God (MRTCG) burst on the scene in a literal explosion that caused a fire that apparently killed 330 members. Curiously, however, the windows of the building in Kanungu where the faithful met their deaths had been boarded over, making it unclear if this was murder or suicide. Further complicating matters was the fact that 6 bodies had been buried near the church prior to the fire. Finally, 444 corpses were exhumed from mass graves at four different locations, suggesting that murder rather than suicide was in play (Mayer 2001, 204). Reporters and cult experts instantly drew comparisons with Jonestown, even noting that the total number of deaths approached that of the 1978 tragedy. Human rights groups in Uganda now say that if police had carried out further exhumations, the number of deaths may have exceeded those in Jonestown (Walliss 2005).

Any parallels between Peoples Temple or other violent NRMs and the MRTCG, however, were merely superficial. Led by female visionaries and Roman Catholic priests, the MRTCG was just one response to the hundreds of reported instances of Marian apparitions sweeping across Africa in the 1990s that comprised a "reformist revitalization movement within the Roman Catholic Church" (Melton and Bromley 2002b, 236). Messages and appearances of the Virgin Mary and Jesus to the twelve apostles leading the MRTCG denounced the sinfulness of the world and called for immediate repentance and a life to be lived in strict adherence to the Ten Commandments. One prophecy saw the cleansing of the earth and the elimination of its inhabitants. Church documents clearly showed that the group expected the end to come sometime in 2000, with a new calendar commencing with "Year One" (Mayer 2001; Melton and Bromley 2002; Mayer 2011). It is evident that members expected something to happen in March, because they spent the days and weeks beforehand getting their affairs in order: selling cattle at bargain rates, paying off taxes and debts, and taking property deeds to the local police department for safekeeping.

Among the various theories for the spectacular ending of MRTCG is the claim that the leaders did not die with the group but merely absconded with members' money. The fraud-and-flight thesis remains a favorite among law enforcement officials, especially since the bodies of the leaders were never identified (Walliss 2014). Another theory was that a series of earlier failed prophecies created overwhelming dissatisfaction that threatened the group; this is also problematic, since predictions consistently centered on the year 2000. External opposition was minimal, and MRTCG generally had good relations with local officials. Another explanation was that disaffected members wanted their property back and were making trouble, so they were killed and the faithful died along with them. Walliss (2014) concluded that internal factors, such as the leaders' perception of persecution, probably played the main role in the "apocalyptic trajectory" that led to the deaths.

Vokes (2009), however, determined that the deaths were in fact mass suicide. He argued that MRTCG was primarily made up of the dispossessed, especially women, and particularly those suffering from AIDS or other poverty-related diseases. A malaria epidemic in 1998 struck the Kanungu camp exceptionally hard, and given the preexisting conditions of its residents, many died. While most of the bodies were buried on-site in mass graves, which the police never examined, a number were transported to and buried at other MRTCG facilities, which were investigated. This would explain the earlier deaths, while clumsy exhumations – during which the bodies were unearthed by tying ropes around their necks – would explain why police thought the victims had been murdered. Malaria deaths due to El Niño conditions, followed by drought and famine due to a La Niña year, combined with "the group's exposure to a global Marian literature which was itself becoming increasingly apocalyptic" (Vokes 2009, 206). Everything served to make the group more millenarian. On the last day, members more or less willingly ingested poison to make it onto the "Ark," in one member's words, before major catastrophes arrived (Vokes 2009, 209–210). They already had little to lose. According to Vokes, a few true believers neatly placed the deceased into a pile before setting fire to it, and to themselves. Photographs seem to show that no explosion occurred and that the fire burned very slowly; though the windows were nailed shut, most of those inside were already dead.

While Vokes (2009) asserted that the deaths in Kanungu were from mass suicide, Walliss (2005) and Mayer (2011) came to more ambiguous conclusions about the MRTCG tragedy. A desire to make an amazing and astounding exit might have been one motivation, given what the MRTCG prophet Credonia Mwerinde (1952–2000?) told her friend: she would be hearing about the group on the radio and reading about it in the newspapers (Mayer 2011). Members wanted friends and family to recollect their dedication and commitment, even if it meant self-sacrifice. Mayer closed by observing that

> The murderous end of the group could have been a radical response to expressions of internal discontent along with a desire to make a radical statement to the world and to force its prophecy to be fulfilled. If the leaders all perished in the event, they had probably managed to convince themselves that they were about to go to heaven – even if this would need some human help and a fire of their own making (Mayer 2011, 212).

The equivocal conclusions regarding MRTCG reflected the difficulties inherent in comparing different occasions of cult violence. Comparative studies have demonstrated the uniqueness, rather than the correspondence, of groups – especially when it came to deadly outbursts. Examinations of lesser-known groups, such as the Ananda Margas of India and their ideology of "perpetual cosmic war" (Crovetto 2008), also problematized grand conclusions, as did reports of murders perpetrated by leaders of ISKCON that occurred in the transitional phase of the Hare Krishnas after the death of Swami Prabhupada (Rochford and Bailey 2006). Furthermore, analyses of historical cases (Jenkins 2000; Wessinger 2000b) and reassessments of contemporary moments of cult violence undermined the axiom that all NRMs are violent (Lewis and Petersen 2005; Lewis 2011; Lewis and Cusack 2014; Lewis and Petersen 2014). The "Big Five" (Lewis 2011) or the "canonical cases" (Barkun 2004) of Jonestown, Waco, Solar Temple, Aum Shinrikyō, and Heaven's Gate (I would add the Movement for the Restoration of the Ten Commandments of God to the canon) did not tell the whole story. Indeed, as Feltmate asks, is violence the defining characteristic of these particular new religions (Feltmate 2016)? With such a variety of beliefs and practices, it seemed inevitable that theoretical diversity should emerge.

7 9/11 Changed Everything: Islam and New Religious Movements

On 11 September 2001, hijackers flew two U.S. passenger jets into the World Trade Center in New York City and a third into the Pentagon in Washington, D.C. Passengers on a fourth plane foiled the hijackers by diverting the jet from its presumed destination, the White House, and deliberately crashing it in rural Pennsylvania. Almost 3,000 people died that day, including 19 hijackers. Members of al Qaeda (in Arabic, "the base") – an international jihadist group established by Osama bin Laden (1957–2011) – saw their suicide attacks as "martyrdom operations." A document entitled "The Last Night" – which described in detail what the presumptive martyr should do before, during, and at the end of such an act – unmistakably indicated that "this act would be one of spiritual worship and not merely mass murder" (Cook 2002, 21).

Although the events of 9/11 took the world by surprise, two decades of prior terror attacks, including a previous attempt on the World Trade Center in 1993, should have been forewarning. (I am using the word "terror" in the sense in which Juergensmeyer employs it: violent events that terrify and "elicit feelings of revulsion and anger in those who witness them" [2017, 152].) A 1992 analysis of terrorism maintained that, since 1968, U.S. citizens and property had been most frequently targeted, and the U.S. State Department reported that 40 percent of all acts of terrorism in the 1990s were aimed at U.S. citizens and facilities (Juergensmeyer 2000, 178–79). Although that proportion has changed in the twenty-first century, with the biggest incidents occurring in Iraq, Afghanistan, and Pakistan and with European nations a handy target, the United States remains a symbol of Western domination and corruption.

Scholarly studies of Islam had repeatedly pointed out the significant growth in Muslim resurgent or revival movements – sometimes called Islamic fundamentalism or militant Islam – since the 1970s. A polymorphous range of groups, issues, strategies, and social and political environments had developed within Islam from the nineteenth throughout the twentieth centuries. Nationalist battles, along with efforts to modernize along Western lines, created rifts between diverse factions and interests. The 1973 war with Israel, though lost by the Arab states, nevertheless fostered a sense of Islamic self-respect (Esposito 1983), as did the embargo on oil exports to the West. Several events in 1979 – the Soviet invasion of Afghanistan, the Sunni seizure of the Grand Mosque in Mecca, and the Iranian Revolution and takeover of the U.S. Embassy in Tehran – all contributed to pride in Muslim identity. A global war against the "crusaders" had already begun well before the twenty-first century.

Other books in the Elements series cover Islam and violence. The pertinent question for this volume is to what extent, if any, can Islamist violence be compared to that of NRMs? Three common threads can be discerned: CAM accusations of terrorist brainwashing, the role played by endogenous determinants, and the part pertaining to exogenous determinants.

As early as 1982, comparisons of the "psychopathology" of cults and terrorism had been made (West 1982), and after 9/11, the CAM immediately drew parallels between cults and Islamist groups, claiming that adherents of militant Islam had undergone mind control at the hands of typical cult leaders (Wright 2009). Current issues of the *International Journal of Cultic Studies* continue to make such comparisons, usually including at least one article linking terrorism with cultism (e.g., Langone 2015). Psychological analyses connected the process of brainwashing with an acceptance of terror as a suitable expression of ideology. The families of John Walker Lindh (the American fighter for the Taliban charged with treason), Richard Reid (the "shoe bomber"), and Zacarias Moussaoui (known as the twentieth hijacker in the 9/11 attacks) all alleged that their relatives had been brainwashed. Sageman (2004) explicitly rejected the brainwashing thesis as applied to jihadist networks, however, arguing instead for a three-pronged process of conversion: social affiliation, progressive intensification of beliefs and faith, and formal acceptance to the jihad.

Sedgwick (2007) weighed the striking similarities in the internal dynamics of NRMs and jihadist groups, though he also noted key differences. Small terror cells, like religious sects, exist in tension with the wider society; they demand enormous commitment on the part of their members; and they limit contact with outsiders, in part, because outsiders may want to jail, if not kill, them. "The isolation from broader social networks that has been so often noted in studies of members of NRMs becomes even greater" (Sedgwick 2007, 18). Other analyses of militant Islamist organizations also emphasized the importance of creating identifiable boundaries for the purpose of generating cultural legitimacy (Piscatori 1994; Williams 1994). Bifurcating the world into good and evil, or pure and impure, places the significance of the movement into fine relief, not just for society at large but also for religious competitors. This kind of exemplary dualism, also found in apocalyptic NRMs, eliminates the possibility of compromise or dialogue, because all encounters are framed in martial terms. A "logic of religious violence" comes out of the belief in a cosmic struggle being played out in history, in which the individual is currently participating in a decisive way (Juergensmeyer 1988, 2017). This is evident in the apocalyptic narrative that recruiters for the Islamic State in Iraq and Syria (ISIS; Syria is sometimes referred to as al-Sham) have created, as presented in the pages of *Dabiq*, the colorful magazine that articulates the ISIS vision for a caliphate and calls for immigration by Muslims into ISIS-controlled areas.

Additional endogenous influences include an apocalyptic religious worldview that may anticipate cosmic war in order to bring about salvation. Rapoport enumerated four waves of modern terrorism, contending that the present wave should be called religious, since religion was "supplying justifications and organizing principles for the New World to be established" (Rapoport 2002, n.p.). Almost by definition, Islamist groups have a transcendent or sacred purpose: these range from Ayatollah Khomeini's "millennial or mystical" goals (Fischer 1983, 166), to al Qaeda's desire to "establish a righteous caliphate" (Kenney 2011, 708), to messianic hopes "manifestly present in the Iranian revolution" (Rapoport 1993, 449). Melton and Bromley went so far as to claim that al Qaeda "is best viewed as a new religious group that has integrated terrorism into its very fabric" (Melton and Bromley 2002a, xiv).

A final endogenous element might be the fragility of a group suffering from internal stresses that sees violence as the only way out of its difficulties (Wessinger 2000a). The use of force may actually signify weakness in the organization or a failing cause: Ian Reader termed this the "pragmatics of failure" (Wessinger 2000b). There seemed to be a scholarly consensus that this was the case with Palestinian suicide bombers (Kenney 2011) and with al Qaeda's 9/11 mission (Rapoport 2002; Al-Rasheed and Shterin 2009, though *pace* see National Commission on Terrorist Attacks 2004). Indeed, some might argue "that the internal tensions in the movement are greater predictors of the group's actions than its interactions with its sworn enemies" (Juergensmeyer 2017, 257).

Exogenous causes demonstrate that, like NRMs, Islamist movements do not exist in a vacuum, but rather respond to provocation. "Revivalist ideas . . . are a response to external and internal stimuli" (Haddad 1991, 4). Esposito (1992) and Williams (1994) agreed that the reactions to Islamist initiatives actually mold Islamist ideology. Ideology changes depending on organizational success or failure (Piscatori 1994). Exchanges between groups and their opponents may either inflame the strife or de-escalate it, since violence is interactive rather than autonomous. Islamist groups are no more monolithic or static than are NRMs, but instead exist in a state of tension with other influences: political, economic, cultural, religious, and personality driven (Esposito 1992).

More scholarly investigation should be conducted to sift through these parallels in greater depth. It seems likely that decades of sociological and anthropological research into NRMs, along with historical case studies, would illuminate contemporary problems. For the time being, the most notable consequence of 9/11 has been to transfer popular anxiety away from cults and toward Islam. Suspicion of marginal religions and the people who practice them – their clothing, customs, habits, and beliefs – is nothing new. It has simply shifted in the West from NRMs to Islam. Yet new religions are also under increasing pressure, and persecution, in many nations today. At the present time, violence is more likely to come from state and non-state actors than from religious believers.

8   The Twenty-First Century: NRMs under Attack

Given the collaborative nature of religious violence, Bromley remarked upon the dearth of investigations into control agents, whether public or private, and advocated paying more attention to "the extent of repression or control of the NRM in the interactive process" (Bromley 2004, 154). Scholars are beginning to fill that lacuna by documenting the worldwide proliferation of aggressive action taken against NRMs (Wright 1995b; Docherty 2001; Beckford and Richardson 2003; Lucas and Robbins 2004; Richardson 2004a; Richardson 2004b; Clarke 2006; Wright and Richardson 2011; Wright and Palmer 2016). These measures include taxing or restricting the activities of adherents of minority religions; closing or destroying religious buildings; sanctioning unofficial mob violence and assassinations targeting religious leaders; and sponsoring incarceration, torture, and execution of members of religious minorities. In fact, government actions in countries like Germany and Russia have even caused some in the CAM "to become concerned about the possible abridgment of religious and other freedoms" (Rudin 2002).

Undoubtedly the most obvious and egregious violence perpetrated against an NRM is the persecution of Falun Gong by the government of the Peoples Republic of China. Founded in 1992 by Master Li Hongzhi, Falun Gong is a qigong group that uses physical and mental exercises not only to achieve good health and mental well-being, but also to realize the highest spiritual truth. In April 1999, faced with repeated rebuffs in their attempt to gain official recognition, 10,000 members of the movement staged a peaceful protest, conducting their qigong workout outside the Zhongnanhai – the walled housing complex for high-ranking Chinese leadership. Three months later, the PRC government banned Falun Gong, labeling it an "evil cult" (*xiejiao*). Less than a year later, according to some estimates, 35,000 practitioners had been detained, 5,000 had been sent to labor camps, 200 had been jailed, more than

200 had died, and 50 had been placed in mental hospitals (Edelman and Richardson 2003). Citing figures from the Dui Hua Foundation, a nongovernmental organization based in San Francisco and Hong Kong, the U.S. State Department asserted in 2015 that more than 2,880 Falun Gong adherents were held in Chinese prisons as of October 2014, up from 2,200 the previous year (U.S. Department of State 2015, 11).

Allegations that Falun Gong prisoners were involuntary organ donors began to emerge in 2006, with release of the Kilgour-Matas Report (Matas and Kilgour 2006). An investigation into these charges conducted by David Matas, a Canadian human rights attorney, and David Kilgour, a former Canadian Member of Parliament, seemed to indicate that organ harvesting was occurring on live prisoners, who were killed during the surgical procedure. Critics claimed that though the findings were based on logical inferences – such as the very short waiting period for kidneys in China as compared with the wait time in places like Canada and the United States – they lacked concrete evidence, so the authors issued a revised version in 2007, titled *Bloody Harvest*, to address this censure (Matas and Kilgour 2007). In 2015, the U.S. Congress relied extensively on the Kilgour-Matas Report in a resolution expressing concern about "persistent and credible reports of systematic, state-sanctioned organ harvesting from non-consenting prisoners of conscience in the People's Republic of China." In testimony before the U.S. Congressional-Executive Commission on China, British journalist Ethan Gutmann estimated that between 2000 and 2008, some 65,000 Falun Gong members "were murdered for their organs" (Gutmann 2015).

Although Falun Gong practitioners have been the most numerous targets for religious persecution in China, other minorities have experienced similar maltreatment. These include ethnic Muslim Uighurs, Tibetan Buddhists, and members of Christian house churches that are not part of the officially recognized Protestant Christian Church in China. In 2016 the Chinese government

> continued to suppress Uighur Muslims in Xinjiang ... [limit-
> ing] parents' rights to include their children in religious activ-
> ities. Authorities evicted thousands of monks and nuns from the
> Larung Gar Buddhist Institute in Tibet before demolishing their
> homes. The government continued to detain, imprison, and
> torture countless religious freedom advocates, human rights
> defenders, and religious believers ... (U.S. Commission on
> International Religious Freedom 2017, 32)

Human rights organizations report that government authorities have shot and killed Uighur Muslims during protests and raids on their homes. In 2016, Chinese officials removed crosses and demolished churches at more than 1,500 locations in Zhejiang Province alone. Ding Cuimei, the wife of church leader Li Jiangong, suffocated to death trying to protect their house church – which the government does not recognize – as bulldozers razed the building. At least three groups are banned by law: Guanyin Method Sec, Zhong Gong, and Falun Gong (U.S. Department of State 2015, 5). An additional number of Christian groups fall into the category of "evil cults," including the Shouters, Eastern Lightning, Society of Disciples, Full Scope Church, and the Unification Church. All of these groups – Muslim, Christian, and Buddhist – are suppressed under the rubric of being religious or violent extremists. Because accounts of torture, physical abuse, harassment, deten-tion, and imprisonment continue, China remains a "country of particular concern" (CPC) for the U.S. State Department under the International Religious Freedom Act of 1998.

Though China's treatment of Falun Gong stands out as the most heinous, violence against new religions is ubiquitous for many reasons, chief among them being the continued strength and presence of religious actors (Robbins 2003). The globalization of some NRMs that nonetheless retain an ethnic identity, such as Sōka Gakkai and Unificationism, makes some groups suspect, as does the perception that other NRMs, such as the Church of Scientology or The Family International, attempt to Americanize local cultures (Beckford 2004). Lucas (2004) claimed that the end of the Cold War, the attacks of 9/11, spectacles of cult violence, a diminution of academic authority regarding NRMs, and resurgent nationalism elevated concerns about safety and security above protection of religious freedoms. It was difficult to generalize, however, with some Western European countries exhibiting relative tolerance (England, Denmark, Italy), some working toward tolerance (Germany and, more recently, Belgium, where the High Court in 2016 refused to order the dissolution of the Church of Scientology), and others working within an anticult framework (France).

Eastern European nations and Russia presented a similarly rocky landscape. Immediately following the fall of Communism, religious groups in Russia were more widely accepted than they are now, with the reassertion of the primacy of the Orthodox Church in Russian culture. Groups such as the Church of Scientology and Jesuit Catholic Christians have had difficulty renewing the registration required to function legally within the country (Richardson, Krylova, and Shterin 2004); and in May 2017, the Russian Supreme Court "liquidated" Jehovah's Witnesses – that is, eliminated or disbanded the group on the charge of its being an extremist organization. Jehovah's Witnesses have reported police breaking into worship services, mobs attacking members, and angry citizens destroying churches and homes. Similar raids and episodes of repression against Jehovah's Witnesses, as well as Uighur Muslims and Protestant Christians, have occurred in Kazakhstan. Once one of the least-restrictive post-Soviet governments in Central Asia regarding religious freedom, the Kazakhstan government promulgated a registration law in 2011 that targeted religious groups. Under the guise of preventing terrorism, police frequently raid services: in January and May 2016, police stormed church buildings and homes of the New Life Pentecostal Church; in May 2017, they broke into the worship services of Baptist Uighurs. Jehovah's Witnesses are frequent objects of attacks and arrests. A tide of legislation limiting the freedom of NRMs and minority religions has passed in Poland, the Czech Republic, Croatia, Uzbekistan, Estonia, Latvia, and Lithuania – even though the constitutions of these nations explicitly protect the right of freedom of conscience, religion, and thought to individuals (Richardson 2004b; Lucas and Robbins 2004).

African nations also painted a mixed picture, at times showing great acceptance of religious pluralism, and at others great bigotry (Hackett 2004). Disagreements arose when a religious group or movement challenged political authority, public interest, or religious power. This explained why, for instance, the governments of Burkina Faso and Togo decided to investigate the activities of non-mainstream religions (Hackett 2004, 158). Four African nations were included in the U.S. State Department's 2016 "Tier 1" list of CPCs: Central African Republic, Eritrea, Nigeria, and Sudan. The government of Eritrea systematically persecuted religious minorities through torture, arbitrary arrests and detentions without charges, prohibitions on worship or religious observances, and regulation of internal affairs (U.S. Commission on International Religious Freedom 2017, 38). Jehovah's Witnesses were particularly vulnerable: their clandestine Bible study meetings were subject to frequent police invasions, and as of December 2016, fifty-four Witnesses were held without charge (U.S. Commission on International Religious Freedom 2017, 41). The government of Sudan under President Omar Hassan al-Bashir has made a highly restrictive interpretation of Shari'ah the law of the land, criminalizing apostasy from Islam. The case of Meriam Yahia Ibrahim Ishag captured international attention in 2014 when she was sentenced to death for converting to Christianity; an appeals court cancelled the apostasy charges, and she fled the country with her husband and two children, one of whom was born while she was in prison.

Western nations are not immune from the global rise in high-risk, military-style police raids against new religions. Wright and Palmer (2016) documented 116 state raids occurring in 17 different countries over the past six decades. Their study centered on incursions in North and South America, Australia, Israel, and Western Europe. The disastrous encounter in 1993 between federal forces and the Branch Davidians in Waco, Texas, was the most lethal, but other raids have had serious repercussions. Police and social welfare agents in the United States, Canada, France, and Germany have stormed communal centers for The Twelve Tribes, a Christian communal group awaiting the Second Coming of Christ, with the expressed purpose of child protection. In 2013, German authorities forcibly removed forty-one children from Twelve Tribes communities in Nördlingen-Klosterzimmern and Wörnitz on charges of child abuse: parents spank their children. Although most courts quickly sent the children home, twenty remained in state custody. Since then, however, some children have come of age or run away and gone back to their families; others turned twelve and were legally recognized as having the right to choose where they wanted to live (they chose to go home); and four cases concerning eleven children, ages five to eleven, were taken up by the European Court of Human Rights. These latter cases remain pending as of this writing.

In a well-publicized 2008 raid on fundamentalist Mormons in Eldorado, Texas – in which law enforcement and state welfare agents seized 439 children living at the Yearning for Zion Ranch – the courts dismissed 424 cases and allowed the children to return home within two months; fifteen cases involving five mothers remained under supervision; and all but one child was eventually returned to her parents (Schreinert and Richardson 2011). While this seemed to be a victory for members of the Fundamentalist Church of Jesus Christ of Latter-day Saints (FLDS), the cost in loss of religious rights and personal privacy was high. In order to regain custody of their children, all of the families had to sign agreements allowing the Texas Department of Family and Protective Services access to their homes on unannounced visits and to submit to medical, physical, and psychological examinations (Schreinert and Richardson 2011).

Wright and Palmer (2016) claimed that the escalation of paramilitary-style raids against NRMs resulted, in part, from new strategies developed by a transnational Anticult Movement. (Since scholars employ the expression "anticult movement," or ACM, to identify an aggressive and invasive approach to NRMs, I will use ACM rather than CAM in the following discussion.) Social deviance has remained one of the major rhetorical claims anticultists made against NRMs and their leaders (Cox 1978; Jenkins 2000; Kaplan 2001; Evans 2011; Palmer 2011). Because they were inherently irrational, the argument went, the only way that cults could attract and retain members was through brainwashing and mind control. This explained why otherwise-normal young adults rejected their parents' values and renounced middle class expectations. Since conversion to cults was defined as a psychiatric problem, medical solutions were necessary (Richardson 2004a; Clarke 2006). But once the legal system disallowed – and the psychological and psychiatric professions repudiated – the pseudoscientific claims that proponents of brainwashing made, the ACM capitalized upon widespread fears about child abuse and reframed cultic threats as poised against children rather than adults (Wright and Palmer 2016). Aided by moral panics about child endangerment – most notably the Satanism scare of the 1980s – the ACM used the media to successfully leverage both public opinion and government agencies to enact measures against NRMs, ostensibly in order to protect children.

Until the Solar Temple deaths in 1994, the nations of Western Europe seemed relatively immune to the alarms sounded by the American ACM, though Beckford (1985) and Melton (2002) documented early precedents of anticult activity there. The OTS murders and suicides jolted into action an incipient anticultism in Europe, just as Jonestown had energized the American

ACM. European cult-watching groups received a big boost from North American anticultists, who consulted with their counterparts at international conferences, on national study commissions, and through seminars with clergy (Swantko 2000; Shupe and Darnell 2001; Rudin 2002; Wright 2002; Robbins 2003; Lucas 2004; Shupe, Bromley and Darnell 2004). The Fédération Européenne des Centres de Recherche et d'Information sur le Sectarisme (FECRIS), a transnational coalition of anticult groups founded in 1994, boasts members from more than thirty countries, five of them outside Europe. These private, nonprofit organizations have capitalized on popular fears and suspicions of new religions: they help generate news stories about the cult menace and thereby spur into action control agents such as law enforcement or social welfare agencies.

France had been, and remains, receptive to anticult influence, with different state ministries created to combat cults, "sectarian danger," or "deviance." The National Assembly legislatively created the misdemeanor of *abus de faiblesse*, literally abuse of weakness and, more colloquially, taking advantage of vulnerability; in effect, the law criminalized "mental manipulation," a euphemism for brainwashing (Palmer 2008). A number of considerations unique to France and French culture illuminated the ferocity of anticult, or anti-*secte*, sentiment there, including the legacy of anticlericalism from the French Revolution; an embrace of a secular society that the Catholic Church monitored; a fear that French culture will be diluted or perverted from within; and a strong dose of anti-American sentiment (Beckford 2004; Introvigne 2004; Palmer 2004). Furthermore, in popular opinion, a *secte* denotes pathological belief; because it is not acting in a free and fair manner, a *secte* is obviously not worthy of religious freedom protections (Hervieu-Léger 2004).

In other countries, the ACM operated outside of government, whereas in France, ACM organizations and actors were integrated into the state machinery as insiders. "Agencies of the State at all levels are fully engaged in the 'fight against cults' and mobilized to such a high degree that it is now necessary to think of France as the only Western country with an official mission to combat cultism" (Beckford 2004, 29). Hostility and mistrust of new religions were therefore built into the very structure of public and private institutions. According to Wright and Palmer (2016), France accounted for almost half of all government raids against new religions, with fifty-seven; the United States was a distant second with fourteen. The Church of Scientology and its church-related businesses have been a major target, being raided more than twenty-one times between 1971 and 2008. The general anti-*secte* climate in France flared into violence against new religions, with several groups receiving bomb threats or being bombed (the Unification Church facility in Paris has been bombed twice since 1974) and leaders and members receiving death threats (Palmer 2002). Multiple terrorist attacks in France, however – including the murders of the staff of *Charlie Hebdo* in 2015 and the Bastille Day attack of 2016 in Nice – have redirected concerns about *abus de faiblesse* to anxiety over Islamic extremism.

North American cult awareness experts have also exerted an influence in Israel, prompting the Knesset to attempt to pass legislation against "harmful cults," which it defined as groups using "methods of control over thought processes and behavioral patterns" (Newman 2016). The proposed law would not only prosecute cult leaders, but would also create conservatorships for parents to gain control over adult children belonging to religions of which they do not approve. The law would essentially legalize deprogramming, which has already begun to occur in Israel, where spiritual seekers are looking to Asian and New Age religions as alternatives to both secularism and Orthodox Judaism. Twenty-three member NGOs of the International Religious Freedom Roundtable expressed opposition to the proposed legislation. In a letter to the Knesset, thirty-two international scholars of new religions also protested the bill, noting that notions of cultic brainwashing and mind control have been discredited by scholars and the courts ("A Letter" 2016).

The letter to members of the Israeli Knesset was just one of the many ways that a variety of research-oriented cult-watching groups organized in order to protect religious liberty. By providing to the public accurate and objective information about new religions, they hoped to counteract the energetic mobilization of the CAM. Though some government agencies and study commissions have explicitly refused to accept scholarly advice (Introvigne 2004), others welcome the insights neutral parties bring to highly charged investigations into new religions. These third-party intermediaries who advocate for unpopular groups have helped some NRMs in their legal battles with state actors, blunting the impact of ACM activists (Richardson 2004a; Shupe, Bromley, and Darnell 2004). Finally, the scholarly *Journal of Religion and Violence* devotes coverage to the manifold expressions of religious violence found in history and around the globe today.

Conclusions

This historiographical investigation has found that the two general predictors of cult violence have remained robust for more than twenty years. The applicability to a variety of groups across time and location has guaranteed the permanence of endogenous and exogenous explanations. At the same time, it must be remembered that these *predictors* were developed *after* incidents of violence. Many groups – in fact, most groups – with these same characteristics do not show any signs of effecting imminent violent outbursts. Still, the fact that scholars are able to find these traits in diverse movements with relative consistency attests to their viability.

Real-world models seem to support rather well the explanations relying upon the endogenous factors of ideology, encapsulation or isolation, and charismatic leadership. An ideology that converts millennial and apocalyptic expectations into actions designed to bring about a new order may supply the impetus to violence. It is possible to recognize the groups that hope for a dramatic transformation of present conditions across a spectrum of beliefs and traditions. Scholars continue to see the isolation of the group as a factor contributing to violent eruptions, with concern about boundaries – geographical or ideological – prevalent in groups that have turned to violence. Complete encapsulation so that the leader might exercise total or totalitarian control existed only in Jonestown, however, though one might claim that the most committed members of Aum Shinrikyō also led severely sequestered lives. Boundary control and the maintenance of purity likewise proved significant among certain militant Islamist groups.

Many analysts saw the leader as exerting a major, even a dominant, influence upon groups. The French antipathy to NRMs emerged in part from a deep suspicion of cult leaders, or *gourous* (gurus), who were assumed to be con artists or closet pedophiles (Palmer 2004). Those in the American CAM also believed charismatic leaders to be crooks, manipulators, psychopaths, and lunatics, concluding that, in whatever guise, they were all up to no good. Though avoiding some of the pejorative language, research-oriented cult watchers who analyzed the leader-follower relationship also determined that the intrinsically unstable nature of charismatic leadership might well be a predictor for cult violence. Dawson (2002) declared that charismatic leadership was indeed a constant in instances of cult violence and identified four problems inherent in a leader retaining legitimacy: maintaining the leader's persona, tempering the effects of follower identification with the leader, handling the routinization of charisma, and achieving new milestones. He concluded that when leaders make wrong choices as they face these challenges, "they can set off a cycle of deviance amplification that greatly increases the likelihood of violent behavior" (Dawson 2002, 81). Oakes (1997) agreed, claiming that if the charismatic leader makes a misstep, violence may result in order for the prophet to avoid facing his or her own failure. When the leader sets impossible goals, followers may also be persuaded to engineer a course of action that leads to violence, such as that which occurred with Aum Shinrikyō (Wessinger 2000a).

Yet most research-oriented scholars were reluctant to dismiss exogenous factors, the second hallmark relating to violence and NRMs, since they served to explain the interaction between groups and their cultural opponents: relatives, apostates and professional anticultists, the news media, and government agencies. These antagonists plainly had an impact on the decision of groups to engage in violence. The relative importance of this interaction, however, was not entirely obvious in all cases. To what extent, for example, did interaction influence the decision to die in Heaven's Gate or in the MRTCG? Nevertheless, a strong resemblance between the actions of ACM organizations and NRMs was undeniable in their general attributes of "single-minded fanaticism, the supreme conviction of their own righteousness, a determination to 'save' individuals from their delusions, and indeed, thereby to 'save the world'" (Wilson 1999, 9). Both the cults and the cult critics modeled exemplary dualism, and the collision between competing worldviews did turn lethal.

The impact of state actors in provoking or even performing violent acts has currently captured the attention of those studying NRMs. In the long history of religion, cult violence is anomalous, while restraints on the free exercise of religion have been the norm. In the past, empires, monarchies, and governments constrained religious activities and fomented persecution, and this trend continues with modern nation-states. The growing number of government-sponsored raids on NRMs and minority religions has increased international concern for religious freedom.

National constitutions of most countries generally affirm some type of religious freedom for individuals, in recognition of the idea that this is a basic human right. The Universal Declaration of Human Rights – to which most nations in the world subscribe – states this explicitly in Article 18. Yet countries are not living up to their own constitutionally mandated requirements when they jail, inhibit, or otherwise harass individuals and groups as they attempt to exercise their constitutionally given freedoms. This breach of a country's law can be seen, for example, in Russia (Richardson et al. 2004) and China (Edelman and Richardson 2003). One of the most blistering critiques of events in Waco demonstrated that the FBI had violated its own negotiation protocols sixteen times (Wright 1999).

Melton and Bromley (2002b) concluded that because violence is inter-active, and because the primary impetus for it may come either from the movement itself or from outside control agents, it may be better to think of dangerous situations rather than dangerous organizations. This seems especially true given the theatrical nature of cult violence. NRMs may well be acting according to an apocalyptic script to stage an event that delivers a compelling, if not always clear, message to an uncomprehending audience (O'Leary 1994; Barkun 2004; Juergensmeyer 2017). Yet state actors may also be performing dramatic parts in order to convey a competing message. Lalasz and Gonzalez (2011) claimed that the raids on the FLDS in Texas could be characterized as "crime control theater" (CCT), in which law enforcement agencies created the illusion of combating lawlessness. Griffin and Miller (2008) developed the theory of CCT in conjunction with their assessment of AMBER alerts designed to notify the public of child abductions. Lalasz and Gonzalez applied similar analytical methods to the 2008 forays against the FLDS, concluding that "although [the raids] may have sounded noble and sensible at the time, they were actually ineffective in investigating, prosecuting, or curtailing the illegal behavior for which they were instigated" (Lalasz and Gonzalez 2011, 194).

Thus, in volatile circumstances, both sides, or all sides, may be following scripted scenarios that inevitably lead to dramatic denouements. When an apocalyptic drama appears on the world stage – as seemed to be the case with ISIS in 2014 and 2015 – "it will be useful to remember that there are numerous possible endings to its story, and not all of them require bloodshed" (O'Leary 1994, 228).

Journalists could contribute to the conciliation process by critically weighing accusations made by all parties with vested interests, not just claims made by NRMs. This means that narratives developed by relatives, apostates, professional cult awareness organizations and individuals, and control agents would receive the same skeptical appraisal as those presented by members of NRMs. Media bias against new and minority religions is well documented (e.g., Beckford 1985; Richardson 1995; Shupe and Hadden 1995; Clarke 2006), and for this reason the news media are rightly included among the cultural opponents aligned against NRMs (Hall 1982, 1987). The media are not neutral transmitters of information but cowriters of dramas that feature heroes and villains and hence have the power to fashion public opinion. History shows that when media reports create sufficient alarm, control agents are forced into action in order to appear responsive to perceived threats (Beckford 1999).

Another step toward reducing the race toward climactic consummations would be to research the occasions where potentially deadly confrontations were averted. Barker (1986) noted that few studies of NRMs made use of control groups for comparison, while Bromley (2004) lamented the fact that nonviolent finales received little scholarly attention. Wessinger (2000a) described how religious studies scholars helped prevent violent outcomes with the Freemen, a Christian Patriot movement in Jordan, Montana, in 1996 and with Chen Tao, an apocalyptic UFO group in Garland, Texas, in 1997. As a former member of The Covenant, The Sword, and The Arm of the Lord, Kerry Noble (2010) described how he contributed to the peaceful resolution of the confrontation between FBI agents and the violent white supremacist group in 1985. In 2016, it appears that the FBI tried to avert a deadly confrontation with Ammon Bundy and extremist Mormons involved in the forty-one day armed occupation of the Malheur Wildlife Refuge in the state of Oregon. What strategies helped to avoid violent blow-ups? What can be learned?

Cult violence will undoubtedly erupt in the future from an unknown group in an unexpected setting. This fact should not serve as the impetus for government surveillance of religions, but rather as the incentive for vigilance by all of the cult-watching groups. If an NRM breaks the law through tax fraud or physical abuse of its members, that is a law enforcement issue that needs reporting to appropriate authorities. If a quasi-religious group takes up arms against ethnic minorities or duly elected governments, that is a military matter requiring multinational consideration and possible intervention.

The fact remains, however, that the great majority of members of new religions simply want to be able to live out their commitment in peace. It may take third-party intervention by human rights organizations, nongovernmental organizations and nonprofit groups devoted to protecting religious liberty and freedom of conscience, religious studies scholars, and other outsiders to defend the rights of unpopular NRMs. It will undeniably require intelligent and measured evaluation of the dramatic scripts by which all of the assorted adversaries operate to forestall future violent incidents.

Appendix

Explanatory Theories about Cult Violence

Barkun 1974: Disaster and the Millennium

Necessary factors for the development of millennial movements include the following:

1. Multiple rather than single disasters.
2. A body of apocalyptic ideas readily available.
3. A charismatic leader who shapes doctrines in response to the disasters.
4. A homogeneous and insulated disaster area.

Barkun, Michael. 1974. *Disaster and the Millennium*. New Haven, CT: Yale University Press.

Levi 1982: Violence and Cohesion

Three factors suggest that there is a link between cohesion and violence:

1. Religious violence is most likely to occur in a highly uncohesive societal context. Times of social change aggravate deprivations that undermine the attraction and therefore the cohesion of future sect members to their society.
2. Religious violence is most likely to be committed by members of a highly cohesive sect. The most violence should therefore occur in authoritarian, totalistic sects.

3. Extreme cohesion leads to violence only when this cohesion gives rise to extremist views. Thus, religious violence is most likely to occur in sects with religious beliefs, rituals, and traditions that explicitly portray homicide or suicide as a means of obtaining sectarian ends.

Levi, Ken. 1982. "Jonestown and Religious Commitment in the 1970s." In *Violence and Religious Commitment: Implications of Jim Jones's People's Temple Movement*, ed. Ken Levi, 3-20. University Park: Pennsylvania State University Press.

Juergensmeyer 1988: The Logic of Religious Violence

There are a great many religious communities in which the language of cosmic struggle justifies acts of violence. The following tenets are found whenever these deeds occur:

1. The cosmic struggle is played out in history rather than a mythical setting.
2. Believers identify personally with the struggle.
3. The cosmic struggle continues in the present.
4. The struggle is at a point of crisis where individual action can make a difference.
5. Acts of violence have cosmic meaning.

Juergensmeyer, Mark. 1988. "The Logic of Religious Violence." In *Inside Terrorist Organizations*, ed. David C. Rapoport, 172–93. New York, NY: Columbia University Press.

Robbins and Anthony 1995: Factors Enhancing the Volatility of Marginal Religious Movements

Three main groups of endogenous (internal) factors contribute to violence:

1. Factors related to the consequences of *apocalyptic* beliefs and fervent millennial expectations.
2. Factors related to the nature and characteristic volatility of *charismatic* leadership.
3. Residual factors that are more loosely interrelated but that might be viewed as relating to the significance of some social movements as communal-ideological *systems* with "boundaries" and systemic problems that may be given different priorities by different groups and leaders, who may attempt to resolve them in different ways.

These groupings do not denote single variables, but ensembles of variables.

Robbins, Thomas and Dick Anthony. 1995. "Sects and Violence: Factors Enhancing the Volatility of Marginal Religious Movements." In *Armageddon in Waco: Critical Perspectives on the Branch Davidian Conflict*, ed. Stuart A. Wright, 236–59. Chicago, IL: University of Chicago Press.

Anthony and Robbins 1997: Religious Totalism and Exemplary Dualism

Totalistic, or authoritarian, movements of a particular kind are volatile and may become engaged in violence if they have the following characteristics:

1. Apocalyptic worldviews.
2. Highly dualistic (quasi-Manichean) and absolutist beliefs.
3. Charismatic leadership.

"Totalist movements with exemplary dualist worldviews and vivid apocalyptic expectations are potentially volatile, particularly if led by charismatic leaders with messianic self-conceptions."

Anthony, Dick and Thomas Robbins. 1997. "Religious Totalism, Exemplary Dualism, and the Waco Tragedy." In *Millennium, Messiahs, and Mayhem:*

Appendix

Contemporary Apocalyptic Movements, ed. Thomas Robbins and Susan J. Palmer, 261–84. New York, NY: Routledge.

Galanter 1999: Suicide, Murder, and Immolation

There are a number of characteristics common to the groups that have practiced violence:

1. There is isolation or distancing themselves from the common culture.
2. The emergence of paranoia and grandiosity in the leader: "The interweaving of grandiosity and paranoia sets the stage for thinking that a fight to the death, or mass suicide, or martyrdom following a confrontation with the government is legitimate."
3. The leader has absolute dominion over the followers.
4. Government mismanagement in the name of religious freedom: "Religious freedom must be respected when the government intervenes, but certain options should be pursued in order to protect a free society from abusive charismatic groups."
5. There is the ideologic theme of death in which murder can be justified as the means to a sanctioned end, "and suicide can be seen as the portal of salvation."
6. A triggering event, which is "a spark that ignites the tinder in groups that carry within their ethos the themes of suicide, killing, or sanctified death."

Galanter, Marc. 1999. *Cults: Faith, Healing, and Coercion*, 2nd ed. New York, NY: Oxford University Press.

Lifton 1999: Features of a World-Destroying Cult

The characteristics of a world-destroying cult like Aum Shinrikyō may be applied to other groups willing to cross the threshold into violence:

Appendix

1. Totalized guruism, which [becomes] paranoid guruism and megalomanic guruism.
2. A vision of an apocalyptic event or events that will destroy the world so that it might be renewed.
3. An ideology of killing to heal – that is, altruistic murder.
4. Relentless efforts at self-purification.
5. The lure of ultimate weapons.
6. A shared state of aggressive numbing, which means total identification with the guru.
7. Extreme technocratic manipulation, along with claims to absolute scientific truth.

Lifton, Robert Jay. 1999. *Destroying the World to Save It: Aum Shinrikyō, Apocalyptic Violence, and the New Global Terrorism*. New York, NY: Metropolitan Books.

Wessinger 2000: Catastrophic Millennial Groups

The characteristics of catastrophic millennial groups that are a cause for concern:

1. Catastrophic millennial beliefs combined with belief in reincarnation and with the members' conviction that the group is being persecuted.
2. The theological conviction that one's home is not on this planet, combined with social alienation due to a sense of persecution and lack of social acceptance.
3. A sense of persecution that is expressed in a belief in conspiracy theories.
4. Catastrophic millennial beliefs that are related to a radical dualistic view of good versus evil that dehumanizes other people.
5. Catastrophic millennial and dualistic beliefs that expect and perhaps promote conflict.

6. The group's resistance to investigation and withdrawal to an isolated refuge and/or a very aggressive battle against its enemies.
7. Followers dependent on a charismatic leader as the sole means to achieve the ultimate concern.
8. Charismatic leader who sets impossible goals for the group.
9. A catastrophic millennial group that gives up on proselytizing to gain converts and turns inward to preserve salvation for its members alone.
10. The above characteristics, combined with membership in a group that demands high exit costs in terms of personal identity, associations, and livelihood.
11. The group's leader giving new identities to the followers, perhaps including new names, and drastically rearranging the members' family and marriage relationships.
12. The group's living in an isolated situation where information about the outside world is controlled by the leader, so that the members are not exposed to alternative interpretations of reality.
13. Relatively small acts of violence repeated in a ritualistic manner so that the scale and intensity of the violence increases.

Wessinger, Catherine. 2000. *How the Millennium Comes Violently: From Jonestown to Heaven's Gate.* New York, NY: Seven Bridges Press.

Bromley and Melton 2002: Dramatic Denouements

Certain violent outcomes are "the product of an interactive sequence of movement–societal exchanges, and these qualities mean that ultimate outcomes remain contingent through the interactive sequence" (1–2).

Bromley identifies four levels of violence, with violence increasing through the process:

1. Latent Tension – in which contradictions between group and society are clear but there is no direct engagement.

2. Nascent Conflict – in which positions are not yet articulated, but adversaries are seen as troublesome.
3. Intensified Conflict – "in which there is heightened mobilization and radicalization of movements and oppositional groups, entry of third parties, and orientation by parties toward one another as 'dangerous'."
4. Dramatic Denouement – in which "subversive" parties lead to "final reckoning intended to reverse power and moral relationships."

Bromley, David G. and J. Gordon Melton, eds. 2002. *Cults, Religion, and Violence*. Cambridge: Cambridge University Press.

Lewis 2005: Suicide Groups

Based on analyses of Peoples Temple, Solar Temple, and Heaven's Gate, the essential characteristics of a suicide group are:

1. Absolute intolerance of dissenting views.
2. Total commitment of members.
3. Exaggerated paranoia about external threats.
4. Leader isolates him/herself or the entire group from the nonbelieving world.
5. Leader's health is failing in a major way, not just a transitory sickness; or, alternatively, the leader believes he or she is dying.
6. No successor and no steps being taken to provide a successor; or, alternatively, succession plans have been frustrated.
7. Group is either stagnant or declining, with no realistic hopes for future expansion.

Lewis, James R. 2005. "The Solar Temple 'Transits': Beyond the Millennialist Hypothesis." In *Controversial New Religions*, ed. James R. Lewis and Jesper Aagaard Peterson, 295–317. New York, NY: Oxford University Press.

Juergensmeyer 2017: Cosmic War (Revised)

Rather than begin with religion, this approach starts with real-life confrontations in the world that may turn to religion and take on the guise of cosmic war:

1. The struggle is perceived as a defense of basic identity and dignity.
2. Losing the struggle would be unthinkable.
3. The struggle is blocked and cannot be won in real time or in real terms but must be reconceived on a sacred plane, where mythical strength is the only resource left.

Juergensmeyer, Mark. 2017. *Terror in the Mind of God: The Global Rise of Religious Violence*, 4th ed. Berkeley: University of California Press.

Acknowledgements

My sincere appreciation goes to the coeditors of this Elements series, Margo Kitts and James R. Lewis. I am honored to be included in this important project. James T. Richardson, John R. Hall, and Catherine Wessinger have provided useful insights, while Massimo Introvigne made very helpful comments on the manuscript. I thank the staff at Cambridge University Press for working with me to improve the final product. And though it is a cliché, it is nevertheless true: eternal gratitude goes to my husband, partner, and friend, Fielding M. McGehee III.

Bibliography

"A Letter to Members of the Knesset." 2016. CESNUR. www.cesnur.org/2016/letter_knesset.htm, accessed January 22, 2018.

Åkerbäck, Peter. 2008. *De obeständiga religionerna: Om kollektiva sjalvmord och frälsning i Peoples Temple, Ordre du Temple Solaire, och Heaven's Gate*. Stockholm: Stockholm University.

Al-Rasheed, Madawi and Marat Shterin. 2009. "Introduction: Between Death of Faith and Dying for Faith. Reflections on Religion, Politics, Society and Violence." In *Dying for Faith: Religiously Motivated Violence in the Contemporary World*, ed. Madawi Al-Rasheed and Marat Shterin, xvii–xxx. London: I. B. Tauris.

Ammerman, Nancy T. 1993. "Report." In *Recommendations of Experts for Improvements in Federal Law Enforcement after Waco*. Washington, D. C.: U.S. Department of Justice.

Anthony, Dick and Thomas L. Robbins. 1978. "The Effect of Détente on the Growth of New Religions: Reverend Moon and the Unification Church." In *Understanding the New Religions*, ed. Jacob Needleman and George Baker, 80–100. New York, NY: Crossroad.

1997. "Religious Totalism, Exemplary Dualism, and the Waco Tragedy." In *Millennium, Messiahs, and Mayhem: Contemporary Apocalyptic Movements*, ed. Thomas Robbins and Susan J. Palmer, 261–84. New York, NY: Routledge.

Appel, Willa. 1983. *Cults in America: Programmed for Paradise*. New York, NY: Henry Holt.

Arjomand, Said Amir, ed. 1984. *From Nationalism to Revolutionary Islam*. Albany: State University of New York Press.

Armstrong, Karen. 2014. *Fields of Blood: Religion and the History of Violence*. New York, NY: Alfred A. Knopf.

Bach, Marcus. 1961 [rep. 1993]. *Strange Sects and Curious Cults*. New York, NY: Barnes and Noble.

Balch, David and David Taylor. 2002. "Making Sense of the Heaven's Gate Suicides." In *Cults, Religion, and Violence*, ed. David G. Bromley and J. Gordon Melton, 209–28. Cambridge: Cambridge University Press.

Bardin, David J. 1994. "Psychological Coercion and Human Rights: Mind Control ('Brainwashing') Does Exist." *Psychological Coercion and Human Rights*. Reprinted by International Cultic Studies Association, at www .icsahome.com/articles/psychological-coercion-and-human-rights-bar din, accessed January 22, 2018.

Barker, Eileen. 1984. *The Making of a Moonie: Choice or Brainwashing*. Oxford: Blackwell.

    1986. "Religious Movements: Cult and Anticult since Jonestown." *Annual Review of Sociology* 12: 329–46.

    2002. "Watching for Violence: A Comparative Analysis of the Roles of Five Types of Cult-Watching Groups." In *Cults, Religion, and Violence*, ed. David G. Bromley and J. Gordon Melton, 123–48. Cambridge: Cambridge University Press.

Barkun, Michael. 1974. *Disaster and the Millennium*. New Haven, CT: Yale University Press.

    2002. "*Project Megiddo*, the FBI, and the Academic Community." In *Millennial Violence: Past, Present, and Future*, ed. Jeffrey Kaplan, 97–108. London: Routledge.

    2004. "Religious Violence and the Myth of Fundamentalism." In *Religious Fundamentalism and Political Extremism*, ed. Leonard Weinberg and Ami Pedahzur, 55–77. London: Frank Cass.

Bibliography

Beckford, James A. 1985. *Cult Controversies: The Societal Response to New Religious Movements*. London: Tavistock Publications.

    1999. "The Mass Media and New Religious Movements." In *New Religious Movements: Challenge and Response*, ed. Bryan Wilson and Jamie Cresswell, 103–19. London: Routledge and the Institute of Oriental Philosophy European Centre.

    2004. "'Laïcité,' 'Dystopia,' and the Reaction to New Religious Movements in France." In *Regulating Religion: Case Studies from around the Globe*, ed. James T. Richardson, 27–40. New York, NY: Kluwer Academic/Plenum Publishers.

Beckford, James A. and James T. Richardson, eds. 2003. *Challenging Religion: Essays in Honour of Eileen Barker*. London: Routledge.

Behrend, Heike. 1999. *Alice Lakwena and the Holy Spirits: War in Northern Uganda 1985–97*. Athens: Ohio University Press.

Bellah, Robert N. 1976. "New Religious Consciousness and the Crises in Modernity." In *The New Religious Consciousness*, ed. Charles Y. Glock and Robert N. Bellah, 333–52. Berkeley: University of California Press.

Bogdan, Henrik. 2011. "Explaining the Murder-Suicides of the Order of the Solar Temple: A Survey of Hypothesis." In *Violence and New Religious Movements*, ed. James R. Lewis, 133–45. New York, NY: Oxford University Press.

Bromley, David G. 2002. "Dramatic Denouements." In *Cults, Religion, and Violence*, ed. David G. Bromley and J. Gordon Melton, 11–41. Cambridge: Cambridge University Press.

    2004. "Violence and New Religious Movements. In *The Oxford Handbook of New Religious Movements*, ed. James R. Lewis, 143–62. New York, NY: Oxford University Press.

Bromley, David G. and J. Gordon Melton. 2002a. "Violence and Religion in Perspective." In *Cults, Religion, and Violence*, ed. David G. Bromley and J. Gordon Melton, 1–10. Cambridge: Cambridge University Press.

Bromley, David G. and J. Gordon Melton, eds. 2002b. *Cults, Religion, and Violence*. Cambridge: Cambridge University Press.

Bromley, David G. and Anson D. Shupe Jr. 1981. *Strange Gods: The Great American Cult Scare*. Boston, MA: Beacon Press.

　　1989. "Public Reaction against New Religious Movements." In *Cults and New Religious Movements: A Report of the American Psychiatric Association*, ed. Marc Galanter, 305–34. Washington, D.C.: American Psychiatric Association.

Chidester, David. 1988. *Salvation and Suicide: An Interpretation of Jim Jones, the Peoples Temple, and Jonestown*. Bloomington: Indiana University Press.

Clarke, Peter B. 2006. *New Religions in Global Perspective: A Study of Religious Change in the Modern World*. London: Routledge.

Cohn, Norman. 1970 [1957]. *The Pursuit of the Millennium: Revolutionary Millenarians and Mystical Anarchists of the Middle Ages*, rev. and exp. New York, NY: Oxford University Press.

Conway, Flo and Jim Siegelman. 1978. *Snapping: America's Epidemic of Sudden Personality Change*. New York, NY: J. B. Lippincott.

Cook, David. 2002. "Suicide Attacks or 'Martyrdom Operations' in Contemporary Jihad Literature." *Nova Religio* 6, no. 1 (October): 7–44.

Cox, Harvey. 1978. "Deep Structures in the Study of New Religions." In *Understanding the New Religions*, ed. Jacob Needleman and George Baker, 122–30. New York: Crossroad.

Crovetto, Helen. 2008. "Ananda Margas and the Use of Force." *Nova Religio* 12, no. 1 (August): 26–56.

Daniels, Ted. 1992. *Millennialism: An International Bibliography*. New York, NY: Garland Publishing.

Dawson, Lorne L. 2002. "Crises of Charismatic Legitimacy and Violent Behavior in New Religious Movements." In *Cults, Religion, and Violence*, ed. David G. Bromley and J. Gordon Melton, 80–101. Cambridge: Cambridge University Press.

Dennis, Edward S. G. Jr. 1993. *Evaluation of the Handling of the Branch Davidian Stand-Off in Waco, Texas, February 28 to April 19, 1993*. Redacted version. Washington, D.C.: U.S. Department of Justice.

Deutsch, Alexander. 1989. "Psychological Perspectives on Cult Leadership." In *Cults and New Religious Movements: A Report of the American Psychiatric Association*, ed. Marc Galanter, 147–62. Washington, D.C.: American Psychiatric Association.

Docherty, Jayne Seminare. 2001. *Learning Lessons from Waco: When the Parties Bring Their Gods to the Negotiating Table*. Syracuse, NY: Syracuse University Press.

Edelman, Bryan and James T. Richardson. 2003. "Falun Gong and the Law: Development of Legal Social Control in China." *Nova Religio* 6, no. 2: 312–31.

Ellwood, Robert S. Jr. 1973. *Religious and Spiritual Groups in Modern America*. Englewood Cliffs, NJ: Prentice-Hall.

Enroth, Ronald. 1979. *The Lure of the Cults*. Chappaqua, NY: Christian Herald Books.

Esposito, John L. 1992. *The Islamic Threat: Myth or Reality?* New York, NY: Oxford University Press.

    ed. 1983. *Voices of Resurgent Islam*. New York, NY: Oxford University Press.

Evans, Martha Bradley. 2011. "The Past as Prologue: A Comparison of the Short Creek and Eldorado Polygamy Raids." In *Saints under Siege:*

Bibliography

The Texas State Raid on the Fundamentalist Latter Day Saints, ed. Stuart A. Wright and James T. Richardson, 25–50. New York. New York University Press.

Federal Bureau of Investigation. 1999. *Project Megiddo*. Washington, D.C.: U.S. Department of Justice.

Feltmate, David. 2016. "Perspective: Rethinking New Religious Movements beyond a Social Problems Paradigm." *Nova Religio* 20, no. 2 (November): 82–96.

Fischer, Michael M. J. 1983. "Imam Khomeini: Four Levels of Understanding." In *Voices of Resurgent Islam*, ed. John L. Esposito, 150–84. New York, NY: Oxford University Press.

Galanter, Marc. 1989. *Cults: Faith, Healing and Coercion*. New York, NY: Oxford University Press.

    1999. *Cults: Faith, Healing, and Coercion*, 2nd ed. New York, NY: Oxford University Press.

Giambalvo, Carol, Michael Kropveld, and Michael Langone. n.d. "Changes in the North American Cult Awareness Movement." www.icsahome.com/articles/changes-in-the-north-american-cult-awareness-movement, accessed January 22, 2018.

Gilmartin, Kevin M. 1996. "The Lethal Triad: Understanding the Nature of Isolated Extremist Groups." At www2.fbi.gov/publications/leb/1996/sept961.txt, accessed January 22, 2018.

Girard, René. 1977. *Violence and the Sacred*. Trans. Patrick Gregory. Baltimore, MD: Johns Hopkins University Press.

    1986. *The Scapegoat*. Trans. Yvonne Freccero. Baltimore, MD: Johns Hopkins University Press.

    2011. *Sacrifice*. Trans. Matthew Pattillo and David Dawson. East Lansing: Michigan State University Press.

Glock, Charles Y. and Robert N. Bellah, eds. 1976. *The New Religious Consciousness*. Berkeley: University of California Press.

Griffin, Timothy and Monica K. Miller. 2008. "Child Abduction, AMBER Alert, and Crime Control Theater." *Criminal Justice Review* 33: 545–52.

Gutmann, Ethan. 2015. "The Anatomy of Mass Murder: China's Unfinished Harvest of Prisoners of Conscience." Testimony before the Congressional-Executive Commission on China. Washington, D.C., at http://ethan-gutmann.com/the-anatomy-of-mass-murder-chinas-unfin ished-harvest-of-prisoners-of-conscience/, accessed January 22, 2018.

Hackett, Rosalind I. J. 2004. "Prophets, 'False Prophets,' and the African State: Emergent Issues of Religious Freedom and Conflict." In *New Religious Movements in the 21st Century: Legal, Political, and Social Challenges in Global Perspective*, ed. Phillip Charles Lucas and Thomas Robbins, 151–78. New York, NY: Routledge.

Haddad, Yvonne Yazbek. 1991. "The Revivalist Literature and the Literature on Revival: An Introduction." In *The Contemporary Islamic Revival: A Critical Survey and Bibliography*, ed. Yvonne Yazbeck Haddad, John Obert Voll, and John L. Esposito, with Kathleen Moore and David Sawan, 3–22. Westport, CT: Greenwood Press.

Hadden, Jeffrey K. and Anson Shupe, eds. 1986. *Prophetic Religions and Politics*, Vol. 1, *Religion and the Political Order*. New York, NY: Paragon House.

Hall, John R. 1982. "The Apocalypse at Jonestown." In *Violence and Religious Commitment: Implications of Jim Jones's People's Temple Movement*, ed. Ken Levi, 35–54. University Park: Pennsylvania State University Press.

1987. *Gone from the Promised Land: Jonestown in American Cultural History*. New Brunswick, NJ: Transaction Books.

1995. "Public Narratives and the Apocalyptic Sect: From Jonestown to Mt. Carmel." In *Armageddon in Waco: Critical Perspectives on the Branch*

Davidian Conflict, ed. Stuart A. Wright, 205–35. Chicago, IL: University of Chicago.

Hall, John R., with Philip D. Schuyler and Sylvaine Trinh. 2000. *Apocalypse Observed: Religious Movements and Violence in North America, Europe and Japan*. London: Routledge.

Hervieu-Léger, Danièle. 2004. "France's Obsession with the 'Sectarian Threat.'" In *New Religious Movements in the 21st Century: Legal, Political, and Social Challenges in Global Perspective*, ed. Phillip Charles Lucas and Thomas Robbins, 49–59. New York, NY: Routledge.

Hyman, Anthony. 1985. "Muslim Fundamentalism." *Conflict Studies* no. 174 (Special issue): 3–27.

Introvigne, Massimo. 2004. "Something Peculiar about France: Anti-Cult Campaigns in Western Europe and French Religious Exceptionalism." In *The Oxford Handbook of New Religious Movements*, ed. James R. Lewis, 206–20. New York, NY: Oxford University Press.

Introvigne, Massimo and Jean-François Mayer. 2002. "Occult Masters and the Temple of Doom: The Fiery End of the Solar Temple." In *Cults, Religion, and Violence*, ed. David G. Bromley and J. Gordon Melton, 170–88. Cambridge: Cambridge University Press.

Jackman, Mary R. 2002. "Violence in Social Life." *Annual Review of Sociology* 28: 376–415.

Jenkins, Philip. 2000. *Mystics and Messiahs: Cults and New Religions in American History*. New York, NY: Oxford University Press.

Johnson, Paul Doyle. 1979. "Dilemmas of Charismatic Leadership: The Case of the People's Temple." *Sociological Analysis* 40, no. 4 (Winter): 315–23.

Jones, Constance A. 1989. "Exemplary Dualism and Authoritarianism at Jonestown." In *New Religious Movements, Mass Suicide, and Peoples*

Temple: Scholarly Perspectives on a Tragedy, ed. Rebecca Moore and Fielding McGehee III, 209–30. Lewiston, NY: Edwin Mellen Press.

Juergensmeyer, Mark. 1988. "The Logic of Religious Violence." In *Inside Terrorist Organizations*, ed. David C. Rapoport, 172–93. New York, NY: Columbia University Press.

2000. *Terror in the Mind of God: The Global Rise of Religious Violence*. Berkeley: University of California Press.

2017. *Terror in the Mind of God: The Global Rise of Religious Violence*, 4th ed. Berkeley: University of California Press.

Kaplan, Jeffrey. 2001. "The Roots of Religious Violence in America." In *Misunderstanding Cults: Searching for Objectivity in a Controversial Field*, ed. Benjamin Zablocki and Thomas Robbins, 478–514. Toronto: University of Toronto Press.

Kenney, Jeffrey T. 2011. "Millennialism and Radical Islamist Movements." In *The Oxford Handbook of Millennialism*, ed. Catherine Wessinger, 688–713. New York, NY: Oxford University Press.

Kerns, Phil, with Doug Wead. 1979. *People's Temple, People's Tomb*. Plainfield, NJ: Logos International.

Kilduff, Marshall and Ron Javers. 1978. *Suicide Cult: The Inside Story of the Peoples Temple Sect and the Massacre in Guyana*. New York, NY: Bantam.

Krause, Charles A. 1978. *Guyana Massacre: The Eyewitness Account*. New York, NY: Berkley Publishing.

La Barre, Weston. 1971. "Materials for a History of Studies of Crisis Cults: A Bibliographic Essay." *Current Anthropology* 12, no. 1: 3–44.

Lalasz, Camille B. and Carlene A. Gonzalez. 2011. "The Large-Scale FLDS Raids: The Dangers and Appeal of Crime Control Theater." In *Saints under Siege: The Texas State Raid on the Fundamentalist Latter Day Saints*, ed. Stuart B. Wright and James T. Richardson, 178–97. New York: New York University Press.

Langone, Michael D. 2015. "Terrorism and Cultic Dynamics." *ISCA Today* 6, no. 1: 13–15.

Lanternari, Vittorio. 1963. *The Religions of the Oppressed: A Study of Modern Messianic Cults*. Trans. Lisa Sergio. New York, NY: New American Library.

Larsen, Egon. 1971. *Strange Sects and Cults: A Study of Their Origins and Influence*. London: Arthur Barker Ltd.

Lasaga, Jose I. 1980. "Death in Jonestown: Techniques of Political Control by a Paranoid Leader." *Suicide and Life-Threatening Behavior* 10, no. 4: 210–13.

Levi, Ken. 1982a. "Jonestown and Religious Commitment in the 1970s." In *Violence and Religious Commitment: Implications of Jim Jones's People's Temple Movement*, ed. Ken Levi, 3–20. University Park: Pennsylvania State University Press.

ed. 1982b. *Violence and Religious Commitment: Implications of Jim Jones's People's Temple Movement*. University Park: Pennsylvania State University Press.

Lewis, James R. 2005. "The Solar Temple 'Transits': Beyond the Millennialist Hypothesis." In *Controversial New Religions*, ed. James R. Lewis and Jesper Aagaard Peterson, 295–317. New York, NY: Oxford University Press.

ed. 1994. *From the Ashes: Making Sense of Waco*. Lanham, MD: Rowman and Littlefield.

ed. 2011. *Violence and New Religious Movements*. New York, NY: Oxford University Press.

Lewis, James R. and Carole M. Cusack, eds. 2014. *Sacred Suicide*. Burlington, VT: Ashgate.

Lewis, James R. and Jesper Aagaard Petersen, eds. 2005. *Controversial New Religions*. New York, NY: Oxford University Press.

Lewis, James R. and Jesper Aagaard Petersen, eds. 2014. *Controversial New Religions*, 2nd ed. New York, NY: Oxford University Press.

Lifton, Robert Jay. 1999. *Destroying the World to Save It: Aum Shinrikyō, Apocalyptic Violence, and the New Global Terrorism*. New York, NY: Metropolitan Books.

Lindt, Gillian. 1981–82. "Journeys to Jonestown: Accounts and Interpretations of the Rise and Demise of the Peoples Temple." *Union Seminary Quarterly Review* 37: 159–74.

Lucas, Phillip Charles. 2004. "The Future of New and Minority Religions in the Twenty-First Century: Religious Freedom under Global Siege." In *New Religious Movements in the 21st Century: Legal, Political, and Social Challenges in Global Perspective*, ed. Phillip Charles Lucas and Thomas Robbins, 341–57. New York, NY: Routledge.

Lucas, Phillip Charles and Thomas Robbins, eds. 2004. *New Religious Movements in the 21st Century: Legal, Political, and Social Challenges in Global Perspective*. New York, NY: Routledge.

Markowitz, Arnold and David A. Halperin. 1984. "Cults and Children: The Abuse of the Young." *Cultic Studies Journal* 1, no. 2: 22–30.

Martin, Walter R. 1965. *The Kingdom of the Cults: An Analysis of the Major Cult Systems in the Present Christian Era*. Minneapolis, MN: Bethany Fellowship.

Marty, Martin E. and R. Scott Appleby, eds. 1993. *Fundamentalisms and the State: Remaking Polities, Economies, and Militance*. Chicago, IL: University of Chicago Press.

Matas, David and David Kilgour. 2006. *Report into Allegations of Organ Harvesting of Falun Gong Practitioners in China*, at http://organharvestin vestigation.net/report20060706.htm, accessed January 22, 2018.

2007. Bloody Harvest: Revised Report into Allegations of Organ Harvesting of Falun Gong Practitioners in China, at http://organharvestinvestiga tion.net/index.html, accessed January 22, 2018.

Bibliography

Materials relating to the Investigation into the Activities of Federal Law Enforcement Agencies toward the Branch Davidians. 1997. House of Representatives, Committee on the Judiciary with the Committee on Government Reform and Oversight. Washington, D.C.: Government Printing Office.

Mayer, Jean-François. 1999. "'Our Terrestrial Journey is Coming to an End': The Last Voyage of the Solar Temple." *Nova Religio* 2, no. 2: 172–96.

   2001. "Field Notes: The Movement for the Restoration of the Ten Commandments of God." *Nova Religio* 5, no. 1 : 203–10.

   2011. "'There Will Follow a New Generation and a New Earth': From Apocalyptic Hopes to Destruction in the Movement for the Restoration of the Ten Commandments of God." In *Violence and New Religious Movements*, ed. James R. Lewis, 191–214. New York, NY: Oxford University Press.

McConnell, Malcolm. 1984. *Stepping Over: Personal Encounters with Young Extremists*. New York, NY: Reader's Digest Press.

Melton, J. Gordon. 1999. "Anti-Cultists in the United States: An Historical Perspective." In *New Religious Movements: Challenge and Response*, ed. Bryan Wilson and Jamie Cresswell, 213–33. London: Routledge and the Institute of Oriental Philosophy European Centre.

   2002. "The Modern Anti-Cult Movement in Historical Perspective." In *The Cultic Milieu: Oppositional Subcultures in an Age of Globalization*, ed. Jeffrey Kaplan and Heléne Lööw, 265–96. Walnut Creek, CA: AltaMira Press.

Melton, J. Gordon and David G. Bromley. 2002a. "Prologue: September 11, Religion, and Violence." In *Cults, Religion, and Violence*, ed. David G. Bromley and J. Gordon Melton, xiii–xx. Cambridge: Cambridge University Press.

2002b. "Lessons from the Past, Perspective for the Future." In *Cults, Religion, and Violence*, ed. David G. Bromley and J. Gordon Melton, 229–44. Cambridge: Cambridge University Press.

2009. "Violence and New Religions: An Assessment of Problems, Progress, and Prospects in Understanding the NRM–Violence Connection." In *Dying for Faith: Religiously Motivated Violence in the Contemporary World*, ed. Madawi al-Rasheed and Marat Shterin, 27–41. London: I. B. Tauris.

Melton, J. Gordon and Robert L. Moore. 1982. *The Cult Experience: Responding to the New Religious Pluralism*. New York, NY: Pilgrim Press.

Mills, Edgar W. Jr. 1982. "Cult Extremism: The Reduction of Normative Dissonance." In *Violence and Religious Commitment: Implications of Jim Jones's People's Temple Movement*, ed. Ken Levi, 74–87. University Park: Pennsylvania State University Press.

Moore, Rebecca. 1985. *A Sympathetic History of Jonestown*. Lewiston, NY: Edwin Mellen Press.

2011. "Narratives of Persecution, Suffering, and Martyrdom: Violence in Peoples Temple and Jonestown." In *Violence and New Religious Movements*, ed. James R. Lewis, 95–111. New York: Oxford University Press.

2016. "Speakers and Resources." *Alternative Considerations of Jonestown and Peoples Temple*, at http://jonestown.sdsu.edu/?page_id=18183, accessed January 22, 2018.

National Commission on Terrorist Attacks. 2004. *The 9/11 Commission Report: Final Report of the National Commission on Terrorist Attacks*, at http://avalon.law.yale.edu/sept11/911Report.pdf, accessed January 22, 2018.

Needleman, Jacob. 1977 [1970]. *The New Religions*. Garden City, NY: Doubleday.

Bibliography

Newman, Marissa. 2016. "MKs Bid to Tackle 'Harmful Cults' that Ensnare 20,000 Israelis." *Times of Israel*. 22 February. www.timesofisrael.com/will-israels-first-anti-cult-legislation-harm-religious-freedom/, accessed January 22, 2018.

Noble, Kerry. 2010. *Tabernacle of Hate: Seduction into Right-Wing Extremism*, 2nd ed. Syracuse, NY: Syracuse University Press.

Oakes, Len. 1997. *Prophetic Charisma: The Psychology of Revolutionary Religious Personalities*. Syracuse, NY: Syracuse University Press.

O'Leary, Stephen D. 1994. *Arguing the Apocalypse: A Theory of Millennial Rhetoric*. New York, NY: Oxford University Press.

Palmer, Susan J. 2002. "France's Anti-Sect Wars." *Nova Religio* 6, no. 1 (October): 174–82.

2004. "The *Secte* Response to Religious Discrimination: Subversives, Martyrs, or Freedom Fighters in the French Sect Wars?" In *New Religious Movements in the 21st Century: Legal, Political, and Social Challenges in Global Perspective*, ed. Phillip Charles Lucas and Thomas Robbins, 61–73. New York, NY: Routledge.

2008. "Field Notes. France's 'War on Sects': A Post-9/11 Update." *Nova Religio* 11, no. 3 (February): 104–20.

2011. "Rescuing Children? Government Raids and Child Abuse Allegations in Historical and Cross-Cultural Perspective." In *Saints under Siege: The Texas State Raid on the Fundamentalist Latter Day Saints*, ed. Stuart B. Wright and James T. Richardson, 51–79. New York: New York University Press.

Patrick, Ted, with Tom Dulack. 1976. *Let Our Children Go!* New York, NY: E. P. Dutton.

Pavlos, Andrew J. 1982. *The Cult Experience*. Westport, CT: Greenwood Press.

Piscatori, James. 1994. "Accounting for Islamic Fundamentalisms." In *Accounting for Fundamentalisms: The Dynamic Character of*

Movements, ed. Martin E. Marty and R. Scott Appleby, 361–73. Chicago, IL: University of Chicago Press.

Rapoport, David C. 1993. "Comparing Militant Fundamentalist Movements and Groups." In *Fundamentalisms and the State: Remaking Polities, Economies, and Militance*, ed. Martin E. Marty and R. Scott Appleby, 429–61. Chicago, IL: University of Chicago Press.

2002. "The Four Waves of Rebel Terror and September 11." *Anthropoetics* 8, no. 1 (Spring), at www.anthropoetics.ucla.edu/ap0801/terror, accessed January 22, 2018.

Reader, Ian. 1996. *A Poisonous Cocktail? Aum Shinrikyō's Path to Violence*. Copenhagen: Nordic Institute of Asian Studies.

2000. *Religious Violence in Contemporary Japan: The Case of Aum Shinrikyō*. Honolulu: University of Hawai'i Press.

Redlinger, Lawrence J. and Philip K. Armour. 1982. "Changing World: Observations on the Processes of Resocialization and Transformations of Subjective Social Reality." In *Violence and Religious Commitment: Implications of Jim Jones's People's Temple Movement*, ed. Ken Levi, 88–102. University Park: Pennsylvania State University Press.

Reiterman, Tim, with John Jacobs. 1982. *Raven: The Untold Story of the Rev. Jim Jones and His People*. New York, NY: E. P. Dutton.

Report to the Deputy Attorney General on the Events at Waco, Texas, February 28 to April 19, 1993. 1993. Redacted version. Washington, D. C.: U.S. Department of Justice.

Repp, Martin. 2011. "Religion and Violence in Japan: The Case of Aum Shinrikyō." In *Violence and New Religious Movements*, ed. James R. Lewis, 147–71. New York, NY: Oxford University Press.

Richardson, James T. 1982. "A Comparison between Jonestown and Other Cults." In *Violence and Religious Commitment: Implications of Jim Jones's*

People's Temple Movement, ed. Ken Levi, 21–34. University Park: Pennsylvania State University Press.

1985. "Psychological and Psychiatric Studies of New Religions." In *Advances in the Psychology of Religion*, ed. L. B. Brown, 209–33. New York, NY: Pergamon Press.

1992. "Mental Health of Cult Consumers: Legal and Scientific Controversy." In *Religion and Mental Health*, ed. John F. Schumaker, 233–44. New York, NY: Oxford University Press.

1995. "Manufacturing Consent about Koresh: A Structural Analysis of the Role of Media in the Waco Tragedy." In *Armageddon in Waco: Critical Perspectives on the Branch Davidian Conflict*, ed. Stuart A. Wright, 153–76. Chicago, IL: University of Chicago.

2004a. "Legal Dimensions of New Religions." In *The Oxford Handbook of New Religious Movements*, ed. James R. Lewis, 163–83. New York, NY: Oxford University Press.

ed. 2004b. *Regulating Religion: Case Studies from Around the Globe*. New York, NY: Kluwer Academic / Plenum Publishers.

Richardson, James T., Joel Best, and David G. Bromley, eds. 1991. *The Satanism Scare*. New York, NY: Aldine de Gruyter.

Richardson, James T., Galina A. Krylova, and Marat S. Shterin. 2004. "Legal Regulation of Religions in Russia: New Developments." In *Regulating Religion: Case Studies from Around the Globe*, ed. James T. Richardson, 247–57. New York, NY: Kluwer Academic/Plenum Publishers.

Robbins, Thomas. 1988. *Cults, Converts and Charisma: The Sociology of New Religious Movements*. Beverly Hills, CA: Sage Publications.

1989a. "The Second Wave of Jonestown Literature: A Review Essay." In *New Religious Movements, Mass Suicide, and Peoples Temple: Scholarly Perspectives on a Tragedy*, ed. Rebecca Moore and Fielding McGehee III, 113–34. Lewiston, NY: Edwin Mellen Press.

1989b. "The Historical Antecedents of Jonestown: The Sociology of Martyrdom." In *New Religious Movements, Mass Suicide, and Peoples Temple: Scholarly Perspectives on a Tragedy*, ed. Rebecca Moore and Fielding McGehee III, 51–76. Lewiston, NY: Edwin Mellen Press.

2002. "Sources of Volatility in Religious Movements." In *Cults, Religion, and Violence*, ed. David G. Bromley and J. Gordon Melton, 57–79. Cambridge: Cambridge University Press.

2003. "Notes on the Contemporary Peril to Religious Freedom." In *Challenging Religion: Essays in Honour of Eileen Barker*, ed. James A. Beckford and James T. Richardson, 71–81. London: Routledge.

Robbins, Thomas and Dick Anthony. 1995. "Sects and Violence: Factors Enhancing the Volatility of Marginal Religious Movements." In *Armageddon in Waco: Critical Perspectives on the Branch Davidian Conflict*, ed. Stuart A. Wright, 236–59. Chicago, IL: University of Chicago.

Rochford, E. Burke Jr. and Kendra Bailey. 2006. "Almost Heaven: Leadership, Decline and the Transformation of New Vrindaban." *Nova Religio* 9, no. 3 (February): 6–23.

Rosedale, Herbert L., Michael D. Langone, Russell H. Bradshaw, and Steve K. D. Eichel. 2015. "The Challenge of Defining Cult." *ICSA Today* 6, no. 3: 2–13.

Roy, Ralph Lord. 1964. "Conflict from the Communist Left and the Radical Right." In *Religion and Social Conflict*, ed. Martin Lee and Martin E. Marty, 55–68. New York, NY: Oxford University Press.

Rudin, A. James and Marcia R. Rudin. 1980. *Prison or Paradise? The New Religious Cults*. Philadelphia, PA: Fortress.

Rudin, Marcia. 1984. "Women, Elderly, and Children in Religious Cults." *Cultic Studies Journal* 1, no. 1: 7–19.

2002. "Twenty-Five Years Observing Cults: An American Perspective." *Cultic Studies Review* 1, no. 1; at www.icsahome.com/articles/twenty-five-years-observing-cults-an-american-perspective, accessed January 22, 2018.

Sageman, Marc. 2004. *Understanding Terror Networks*. Philadelphia: University of Pennsylvania Press.

Saiedi, Nader. 1986. "What Is Islamic Fundamentalism?" In *Prophetic Religions and Politics*, Vol. 1, *Religion and the Political Order*, ed. Jeffrey K. Hadden and Anson Shupe, 173–95. New York, NY: Paragon House.

Saliba, John A. 1990. *Social Science and the Cults: An Annotated Bibliography*. New York, NY: Garland Publishing.

Scheflin, Alan W. and Edward M. Opton Jr. 1978. *The Mind Manipulators*. New York, NY: Paddington Press.

Schreinert, Tamatha L. and James T. Richardson. 2011. "Pyrrhic Victory? An Analysis of the Appeal Court Opinions concerning the FLDS Children." In *Saints under Siege: The Texas State Raid on the Fundamentalist Latter Day Saints*, ed. Stuart A. Wright and James T. Richardson, 242–63. New York: New York University Press.

Sedgwick, Mark. 2007. "Jihad, Modernity, and Sectarianism." *Nova Religio* 11, no. 2 (November): 6–27.

Shupe, Anson, David G. Bromley, and Susan E. Darnell. 2004. "The North American Anti-Cult Movement: Vicissitudes of Success and Failure." In *The Oxford Handbook of New Religious Movements*, ed. James R. Lewis, 184–205. New York, NY: Oxford University Press.

Shupe, Anson and Susan E. Darnell. 2001. "Agents of Discord: The North American–European Anticult Connection." Paper presented at the Center for the Study of New Religions, International Conference, at www.cesnur.org/2001/CAN1/index.htm, accessed January 22, 2018.

Shupe, Anson and Jeffrey K. Hadden. 1995. "Cops, News Copy, and Public Opinion: Legitimacy and the Social Construction of Evil in Waco."

In *Armageddon in Waco: Critical Perspectives on the Branch Davidian Conflict*, ed. Stuart A. Wright, 177–202. Chicago, IL: University of Chicago.

Shupe, Anson D. Jr. 1982. "Shaping the Public Response to Jonestown: People's Temple and the Anticult Movement." In *Violence and Religious Commitment: Implications of Jim Jones's People's Temple Movement*, ed. Ken Levi, 105–32. University Park: Pennsylvania State University Press.

Shupe, Anson D. Jr. and David G. Bromley. 1980. *The New Vigilantes: Deprogrammers, Anti-Cultists and the New Religions*. Beverly Hills, CA: Sage Publications.

Shupe, Anson D. Jr., Roger Spielmann, and Sam Stigall. 1978. "Deprogramming: The New Exorcism." In *Conversion Careers: In and Out of the New Religions*, ed. James R. Richardson, 145–60. Beverly Hills, CA: Sage Publications.

Singer, Margaret with Janja Lalich. 2003 [1995]. *Cults in our Midst*, rev. ed. San Francisco, CA: Jossey-Bass.

Smith, Archie Jr. 1982. *The Relational Self: Ethics and Therapy from a Black Church Perspective*. Nashville, TN: Abingdon Press.

Smith, Jonathan Z. 1982. *Imagining Religion: From Babylon to Jonestown*. Chicago, IL: University of Chicago Press.

Stark, Rodney and William Sims Bainbridge. 1985. *The Future of Religion: Secularization, Revival, and Cult Formation*. Berkeley: University of California Press.

Stoner, Carroll and Jo Anne Parke. 1977 [1979]. *All Gods Children: The Cult Experience – Salvation or Slavery?* New York, NY: Penguin.

Swantko, Jean A. 2000. "The Twelve Tribes' Communities, the Anti-Cult Movement, and Government's Response." *Social Justice Research* 12, no. 4: 341–64.

Bibliography

Tabor, James D. and Eugene V. Gallagher. 1995. *Why Waco? Cults and the Battle for Religious Freedom in America*. Berkeley: University of California Press.

Thielmann, Bonnie with Dean Merrill. 1979. *The Broken God*. Elgin, IL: David Cook Publishing.

Ulman, Richard Barrett and Wilfred Abse. 1983. "The Group Psychology of Mass Madness: Jonestown." *Political Psychology* 4, no. 4: 637–61.

U.S. Commission on International Religious Freedom. 2017. "Annual Report." Washington, D.C., at www.uscirf.gov/sites/default/files/2017. USCIRFAnnualReport.pdf.

U.S. Department of State. 2015. "International Religious Freedom Report: China." Bureau of Democracy, Human Rights and Labor. Washington, D.C., at www.state.gov/documents/organization/256309.pdf.

Vokes, Richard. 2009. *Ghosts of Kanungu: Fertility, Secrecy, and Exchange in the Lakes of East Africa*. Woodbridge, Suffolk: James Currey.

Wallace, Anthony. 1956. "Revitalization Movements." *American Anthropologist*, New Series 58, no. 2: 264–81.

Wallis, Roy. 1975. "Introduction." In *Sectarianism: Analyses of Religious and Non-Religious Sects*, ed. Roy Wallis, 9–14. New York, NY: John Wiley.

Walliss, John. 2005. "Making Sense of the Movement for the Restoration of the Ten Commandments of God." *Nova Religio* 9, no. 1: 49–66.

    2014. "Apocalypse in Uganda: The Movement for the Restoration of the Ten Commandments of God One Decade On." In *Sacred Suicide*, ed. James R. Lewis and Carole M. Cusack, 109–27. Burlington, VT: Ashgate.

Weightman, Judith Mary. 1984. *Making Sense of the Jonestown Suicides: A Sociological History of Peoples Temple*. Lewiston, NY: Edwin Mellen Press.

Wessinger, Catherine. 1997. "Millennialism with and without the Mayhem." In *Millennium, Messiahs, and Mayhem: Contemporary Apocalyptic*

Movements, ed. Thomas Robbins and Susan J. Palmer, 47–59. New York, NY: Routledge.

2000a. *How the Millennium Comes Violently: From Jonestown to Heaven's Gate*. New York, NY: Seven Bridges Press.

2000b. *Millennialism, Persecution, and Violence: Historical Cases*. Syracuse, NY: Syracuse University Press.

2011. "Millennial Glossary." In *The Oxford Handbook of Millennialism*, ed. Catherine Wessinger, 717–23. New York, NY: Oxford University Press.

2016. "Branch Davidians (1982–2006)." *World Religions and Spirituality*, at https://wrldrels.org/2016/02/25/branch-davidians-2/, accessed January 22, 2018.

West, Louis Jolyon. 1982. "Cults, Liberty, and Mind Control." In *The Rationalization of Terrorism*, ed. David C. Rapoport and Yonah Alexander, 101–7. Frederick, MD: University Publications of America.

1990. "Persuasive Techniques in Contemporary Cults: A Public Health Approach." *Cultic Studies Review* 4, no. 2: 19–33.

White, Mel, with Paul Scotchmer and Marguerite Shuster. 1979. *Deceived*. Old Tappan, NJ: Fleming H. Revell.

Williams, Rhys S. 1994. "Movement Dynamics and Social Change: Transforming Fundamentalist Ideology and Organizations." In *Accounting for Fundamentalisms: The Dynamic Character of Movements*, ed. Martin E. Marty and R. Scott Appleby, 785–833. Chicago, IL: University of Chicago Press.

Wilson, Bryan. 1970. *Religious Sects: A Sociological Study*. London: World University Library.

1999. "Introduction." In *Religious Movements: Challenge and Response*, ed. Bryan Wilson and Jamie Cresswell, 1–11. London: Routledge and the Institute of Oriental Philosophy European Centre.

94

Bibliography

Wooden, Kenneth. 1981. *The Children of Jonestown*. New York, NY: McGraw-Hill.

Worsley, Peter. 1968. *The Trumpet Shall Sound: A Study of "Cargo" Cults in Melanesia*. New York, NY: Schocken Books.

Wright, Stuart A. 2002. "Public Agency Involvement in Government-Religious Movement Confrontations." In *Cults, Religion, and Violence*, ed. David G. Bromley and J. Gordon Melton, 102–22. Cambridge: Cambridge University Press.

　2009. "Reframing Religious Violence after 9/11: Analysis of the ACM Campaign to Exploit the Threat of Terrorism." *Nova Religio* 12, no. 4 (May): 5–27.

　ed. 1995a. "Introduction: Another View of the Mt. Carmel Standoff." In *Armageddon in Waco: Critical Perspectives on the Branch Davidian Conflict*, ed. Stuart A. Wright, xiii–xxvi. Chicago, IL: University of Chicago.

　ed. 1995b. *Armageddon in Waco: Critical Perspectives on the Branch Davidian Conflict*. Chicago, IL: University of Chicago.

　1999. "Anatomy of a Government Massacre: Abuses of Hostage Barricade Protocols during the Waco Standoff." *Terrorism and Political Violence* 11, no. 2 (Summer): 39–68.

Wright, Stuart A. and Susan J. Palmer, eds. 2016. *Storming Zion: Government Raids on Religious Communities*. New York, NY: Oxford University Press.

Wright, Stuart A. and James T. Richardson, eds. 2011. *Saints under Siege: The Texas State Raid on the Fundamentalist Latter Day Saints*. New York, NY: New York University Press.

Wuthnow, Robert. 1976. *The Consciousness Reformation*. Berkeley: University of California Press.

Zeller, Benjamin E. 2011. "The Euphemization of Violence: The Case of Heaven's Gate." In *Violence and New Religious Movements*, ed. James R. Lewis, 173–89. New York, NY: Oxford University Press.

    2014. *Heaven's Gate: America's UFO Religion*. New York: New York University Press.

Zurcher, Louis A. 1982. "A Self-Concept for Religious Violence." In *Violence and Religious Commitment: Implications of Jim Jones's People's Temple Movement*, ed. Ken Levi, 57–74. University Park: Pennsylvania State University Press.

Cambridge Elements

Religion and Violence

James R. Lewis
University of Tromsø

James R. Lewis is Professor of Religious Studies at the University of Tromsø, Norway and the author and editor of a number of volumes, including *The Cambridge Companion to Religion and Terrorism*.

Margo Kitts
Hawai'i Pacific University

Margo Kitts edits the *Journal of Religion and Violence* and is Professor and Coordinator of Religious Studies and East-West Classical Studies at Hawai'i Pacific University in Honolulu.

ABOUT THE SERIES:
Violence motivated by religious beliefs has become all too common in the years since the 9/11 attacks. Not surprisingly, interest in the topic of religion and violence has grown substantially since then. This Elements series on Religion and Violence addresses this new, frontier topic in a series of ca. fifty individual Elements. Collectively, the volumes will examine a range of topics, including violence in major world religious traditions, theories of religion and violence, holy war, witch hunting, and human sacrifice, among others.

ISSNs: 2397-9496 (online), 2514-3786 (print)

Cambridge Elements

Religion and Violence

Printed in the United States
By Bookmasters